A DIFFERENT VISION

A DIFFERENT VISION

The English in Quebec in the 1990s

REED SCOWEN

Maxwell Macmillan Canada

Canadian Cataloguing in Publication Data

  Scowen, Reed, 1931-
    A different vision

  ISBN 0-02-954010-0

  1. Canadians, English-speaking — Quebec (Province),*
  I, Title.

FC2950.5.S29   1991   971.4′004112   C91-093150-X
F1055.E55S29   1991

Maxwell Macmillan Canada
1200 Eglinton Avenue East, Suite 200
Don Mills, Ontario
M3C 3N1

ISBN 0.02.954010.0

Printed and bound in Canada

CONTENTS

FOREWORD

This is a book for English Quebecers. Its purpose is to stimulate further reflection on our future as a community.

The English community in Quebec is declining in numbers and in strength. There are various ways to measure this decline, but everyone would agree that it is taking place. We have lost 110,000 people—15 percent of the community—in fifteen years. In the same period, its proportion of Quebec's population has dropped from 13 percent to 10 percent.[1] Among those who are concerned about this situation, one can distinguish three approaches.

Some say the continued decline is inevitable. They plan to stay in Quebec, but they expect that their children probably will not. They accept this, and would argue that the most responsible role for the leadership of the English community is to ensure that the process is delayed as long as possible and managed in a civilized way, to minimize the hardship for those who will not, or cannot, leave.

Others maintain that there is a long-term place for the English in Quebec, *so long as they can speak French and are willing to do so normally in public,* for example, in their workplaces and on the street. Such an attitude would make them "responsible" English-speaking Quebecers and ensure the "social peace" that will only be possible when their French-speaking neighbours are freed from the insecurity caused by the presence of the English language in their daily lives.

9

Under the terms of this second approach there is no place in Quebec society, over the long term, for a unilingual English-speaking person, or for a bilingual person who chooses to speak English, regularly, outside his private life. Such people would not, of course, be refused admission, but the leadership of the English community would not encourage them.

A third group is more confrontational. They see the English as victims of an unjust government and an exaggerated nationalism and believe that the English community should "fight for its rights," often without having a very clear idea of where this fight might lead us.

This book proposes a fourth approach. I think the English community in Quebec should grow. Furthermore, I believe it can—in confidence, in numbers, and in strength. And I think that the French majority can grow at the same time. In other words, I believe that there is plenty of room in Quebec for both communities, and that it need not be a matter of winners and losers. We can both become stronger together. When this notion is finally accepted, Quebec will be a better place to live and a more powerful participant in the world community, many of whose other members are faced with very similar problems.

In order for all this to happen, the English will have to reassert themselves in a different and positive way, relying on their unique strengths as the distinct society within Quebec that they have always been. Such an approach will make it possible for them eventually to become fully accepted partners in Quebec life. In the meantime, it will enable them to grow in numbers and in confidence through the use of their own resources.

If this book falls into the hands of some French-speaking Quebecers, I would ask them to remain seated until the end of the performance. Those who fear for the future of French Quebec will find nothing in the following pages to justify either indignation or exasperation. This is a peaceful book. I do propose that we no longer co-operate with the French majority in weakening the English community. However, this is not a plan to turn back the clock, but rather to begin a new day.

The English are a small group in Quebec who are trying "to get their act together," and it seems to me that it's time for us to try something new. Even if every English Quebecer were to accept the proposals in this book (and assuming that the diagnosis turned out to be correct), Quebec might find itself with 120,000 more English-speaking people by the end of the century, in a total population of nearly seven million.

The first part of this book, chapters 1 to 4, briefly summarizes what has happened to the English during the past fifteen years and attempts to draw some lessons from the experience. In the firm belief that no one can see clearly through a curtain of hostility, it is written from the premise that there is no blame to be attached to anyone for what has happened. The events, action and reaction, simply need to be understood, and the necessary conclusions drawn from them.

The second part of the book, chapters 5 and 6, is an effort to stimulate the necessary redefinition of the English-speaking community of Quebec in the light of its new situation.

The final chapter is a brief reflection on the climate necessary for the essential future collaboration between the two language communities of Quebec.

This is not a book about Canada or about Quebec's present or future role in the federation. It is just about Quebec. The issues at stake are the same, in my opinion, wherever the current debate on the political status of Quebec may lead and regardless of Quebec's relationships with other provinces, central governments, and sovereign states. They are, for the most part, applicable even to an independent Quebec. The issues are really about the relationship between people and government in a civil society, and I think the subject deserves a book of its own.

Those who have been involved in Quebec's language debate know that the dictionary is often a poor tool in helping to decide which words to use. Many of the expressions used in this book carry a particular emotive charge and have special meanings when used in Quebec, so one or two explanations are in order before we begin.

The words "anglophone" and "francophone" do not appear in this book, except in quotations. Very few English-speaking Canadians feel comfortable with these expressions, which have come into common, and usually incorrect, usage only in the past few years. To replace them, and to avoid cumbersome repetition, the expressions "members of the English-speaking community," "English-speaking Quebecers," "English Quebecers," and "the English" have been used interchangeably. In this book, they all mean the same thing. The definition may be found on page 64. The same practice has been used in the case of "the French."

There are various ways of referring to the state in Quebec. I call Quebec a province, its government a provincial government, and its leader the premier, because these are the correct terms in Canada and to avoid confusion with the corresponding institutions in Ottawa.

A number of quotations in the text and in the footnotes have been translated from their French originals by the author.

The quotations at the beginning of each chapter are from William Shakespeare's story of Henry V. The important thing in this story is not Agincourt, but the universal message that wars resolve nothing and that relationships between English and French can be resolved in a harmonious way.

In the preparation of this book I have been helped by eleven friends who have been kind enough to read the manuscript,

13

make valuable comments on it, and help me locate a number of the references. I would like to express my thanks to them. The book is dedicated to my family.

1

THE NEW COMMUNITY

. . . the Prince our master
Says that you savor too much of your youth,
Desires you let the dukedoms that you claim
Hear no more of you.

Henry V
Act I, scene ii

Majority to Minority

The English of Quebec are in an unusual, almost unique situation. Nearly three-quarters of a million in number, they are part of the most important language group in the world, one that has a virtual monopoly on power in North America.

In Quebec, however, the English are a minority and unlike the English-speaking minorities in other parts of the world (France, for example), they are not expatriates living here temporarily, without supporting institutions and in isolation from the majority group. In Quebec the English are an "indigenous" people, or at least as "indigenous" as the French.

But for 83 percent of the population of Quebec, French is the first language, and the provincial government, which has substantial powers within the Canadian federation, works almost exclusively in that language and openly encourages the expansion of the French-speaking majority. The English of Quebec know what it is like to be members of a minority group.

Many English-speaking people find it hard to accept this state of affairs, and most of them don't really have to. They can leave, or at least their children can. The rest of the country and the continent are rich in opportunities of all kinds for those who speak English.

However, many remain because it is their home, and others arrive because they like the place or because their work brings them there. English Quebecers once made up over 20 percent of the population; today the figure is about 10 percent. They have shared this territory with the French for almost 250 years, and linguistic tensions have existed with varying degrees of intensity during all this time.

The story of these tensions, of course, is the most important chapter in the history of Canada, and we will not tell it again here. Two groups using two powerful languages and occupying the same political space have defined the country, made it rich and interesting, and created many of its problems. Canada is a place founded by two language minorities. In the country as a whole, the French are the minority group; in Quebec, the English.

Minorities are a source of constant trouble for the modern nation-state. Governments seek a sense of common purpose; minorities insist on their right to be different. When a minority defines itself in terms of language, colour, or religion, the debate can become particularly intense. If such a group has its own territorial base, the situation frequently becomes explosive.

Nevertheless most democratic governments, inspired or intimidated by appeals to basic human rights, have adopted a policy of tolerance toward their minorities. Some have gone further and adopted charters or laws that protect these groups and even encourage their expansion.

In other cases, however, the majority has adopted legislative or administrative practices to discourage, limit, and in some cases even eliminate a minority group along with its distinctive characteristics. The Jews, the Asians in Africa, the Native peoples in North America, and the French in Manitoba are only a few of the groups who have been, at one time or another, victims of the unequal battle between the authorities and the "stranger."

In Quebec, the "strangers" are the English and for the past fifteen years the government has attempted to limit the growth and activities of the English-speaking community because its mother tongue is not the language of the majority.

The Quebec population has always been massively French-speaking, and its numerical superiority has increased over the past fifty years. Nevertheless, the strength of the English language in North America and the economic power of the English minority in Quebec have alarmed the political elite and some elements of the population. They have concluded that the "English" language and its community, though small, must be controlled and their expansion limited. This determination arises partly out of anger at the past, partly from fear for the future.

As a result, a number of "language laws" have been proposed, debated, adopted, repealed, and readopted over the past twenty

17

years in a process that has been unendingly controversial. Among the subjects covered by these laws have been public-sector matters such as the language used by the legislature, the courts, the public administration, and in education and health services.

However, in Quebec successive governments have legislated the use of language in the private sector as well—in the workplace, in consumer information and protection, and on public signs. Each of these initiatives has met with resistance from the English community. But it can be fairly said that a majority of the community has come to recognize the pertinence of the concerns expressed by the French of Quebec. And so, efforts at accommodation have been made.

The need for this accommodation was driven home with particular force in November 1976, when a new and radical government, the Parti Québécois, was elected with a promise to create an independent, linguistically homogeneous French-speaking state in Quebec. One element of its program was to reinforce the controversial restrictions on the use of English that had already been established by the previous Liberal government.

Although the Parti Québécois failed to realize its goal of an independent state, it kept its promises on language reform. In 1977 the Charter of the French Language, commonly known as Bill 101, became law. Unique in the free world, it announced a massive intervention in a wide range of language activities and established administrative measures to ensure that this intervention would succeed. For example, individual citizens were invited to help enforce the law, and measures were adopted to encourage them to report infractions by their neighbours.

Bill 101 was a major event in the lives of the English of Quebec. We shall take a very brief look at how it came about.

A New Situation

Those unfamiliar with the political landscape of Quebec should note that since the early 1970s (the period that will concern us for the rest of this book), there have been for all practical purposes only two political parties in Quebec.

The Quebec Liberal Party has been in existence since Confederation. Closely associated, at least until recently, with the federal party of the same name, it has governed Quebec for more than sixty years of the present century. Ideologically, apart from its roots in traditional liberalism, it has been committed to Quebec's membership in the federal system and to a range of policies that, until the emergence of the Parti Québécois, were as far to the left of centre as the Quebec electorate could comfortably tolerate.

The second political party, the Parti Québécois, was founded by René Lévesque in 1968. It has as its *raison d'être* the creation of an independent state in Quebec. A mixture of *independantists* drawn from all shades of the political spectrum, its political programs have generally been to the left of those of the Liberal Party and, until recently at least, expounded a conception of social democracy broadly based on a European model. Its goal of independence has always been fuelled by the idea of a "French" state in North America and by the belief that the French-speaking majority in Quebec could only evolve in its own way, "normally," if it were freed from membership in the Canadian federation, in which many of the essential powers remain in the hands of a central government dominated by an English-speaking majority.

The language issue, however, predated the Parti Québécois. It has always been a preoccupation of French-speaking Quebecers, the most durable of North American minorities. In fact, the creation of the Dominion of Canada as a federal state in 1867 was a response to the determination of French Canadians to retain their language and institutions.

The most recent chapter in the language debate began in the early 1960s with a celebrated clash over the choice of schools for the children of Italian immigrants in Montreal. This event was followed by some very unpopular efforts at language legislation by the Union Nationale government of the time, which was defeated at the polls in 1970. These events raised the political consciousness of the population to a high level and set the stage for what was to come.

The Liberal government that replaced the Union Nationale took a pragmatic approach to the problem. In 1972 it received the final report of a commission it had established to examine in detail the condition of the French language in Quebec. The Gendron Report[2] (named after the commission's president) concluded that French was faced with encroachment by English in almost every sphere of activity. It proposed, in response, a series of far-reaching legislative measures to protect and strengthen the French language. The Gendron Report became the justification and basis for the Liberal Party's language legislation, Bill 22, and for all of the language laws that followed in the years ahead.

The Liberals, with Robert Bourassa as premier, were in power in Quebec from 1970 to 1976. Bill 22 was their major attempt to address the language question. The debates that accompanied the bill's adoption were unclear and often contradictory, reflecting, within the Liberal Party, a passionate conflict over what, if anything, should be done. The members of the party found that the liberal concept of individual rights mixed uneasily with the kind of collective affirmation made explicit in a law that limited the use of someone else's language. Failure to resolve the language issue was one cause of the Liberals' 1976 defeat by the Parti Québécois.

However, even in opposition, where it was to find itself for the next nine years, the Liberal Party remained the only viable political alternative to the separatist government that had taken power. It thus became the focal point of the effort to keep Quebec in Canada and to reach an accommodation between the province's French and English communities.

In 1977 the newly elected Parti Québécois government adopted Bill 101, the Charter of the French Language. Intimately associated with the idea of political independence, the bill transformed language legislation from the exercise in social engineering that it had been under the Liberals into the principal icon of a new faith called "sovereignty-association."

As in most religions, its members held various opinions about the precise configuration of paradise. But on one thing most French Quebecers quickly agreed: Bill 101 made the French language secure; it was good and it should not be touched. Today, fourteen years later, this conviction is even more profoundly held. The very words "Bill 101" have acquired a symbolic value. The law is now supported by all political parties, and no government dares even to amend those parts of it that have since been invalidated by decisions of the Supreme Court of Canada.[3]

In the preamble to this charter it was declared that French was to become "*the language of government and the law as well as the normal and everyday language of work, instruction, communication, commerce and business.*"

Taken at its face value the realization of such an objective is clearly beyond the power of a provincial government in Canada. For that matter, no government in a democratic society could accomplish it. But such was the force of the preamble that it soon acquired an aura that transported it beyond the realm of analysis and into a category of certainties that one normally associates with the telephone directory. For many Quebecers the province was made French, and remains French today, simply by virtue of the declaration itself.

Understandably, such a vision was unacceptable to the English community. Many of the measures proposed in the Charter were unacceptable as well, especially the sections declaring that the Quebec legislature and the courts were to function only in French, and the severe limitations placed on access to English schools. Most objectionable of all, at the emotional level, was section 58, the "signs law," which stated that in commerce and business "public signs and posters and commercial advertising shall be solely in the official language."

The English in 1977

It is difficult today to recall the level of discouragement that existed within the English community in Quebec when Bill 101 was adopted in 1977. The Parti Québécois had just been swept into power on a wave of euphoria that had no precedent in living memory. For the members of the new government and its supporters everything seemed possible, even inevitable, including the creation of an independent Quebec based on the principles and experience of social democracy in Europe.

The Liberal government and the Liberal Party, which most English Quebecers had traditionally supported, were left in almost total disarray. The premier, Robert Bourassa, had been defeated in his own riding and had resigned. He left behind twenty-six members of the opposition in a legislature with 110 seats, representing a political party that lacked the faintest idea of where to turn for leadership or direction.

The rest of Canada was in a state of shock as well. Numerous patriotic groups sprang up across the country, each proposing to show French-speaking Quebec that it was loved and needed and asking, "What does Quebec want?" The prime minister of Canada appointed a special task force (the Pepin–Robarts Commission)[4] to travel to every corner of the country and make recommendations on establishing a new political order that would restore "national unity."

English-speaking Quebecers were on the front lines throughout all this. Some observers saw them as the cause of all the trouble, others as innocent victims. For those who were not observers, but living the experience, it seemed as if a whole way of life, not just a government, had changed. An exodus began, mainly to Ontario. From 1976 to 1986 the net emigration from Quebec to other parts of Canada was 236,000, and of those emigrants 147,000 (62 percent) were English-speaking.[5] Even allowing for new arrivals from outside Canada,

Quebec's English community was reduced by 15 percent in only ten years.

Large Quebec businesses whose activities covered the whole of Canada, controlled largely by English-speaking Quebecers, began to move out of the province. Corporate decision-makers transferred entire head offices and their staff, some, like the Bank of Montreal, discreetly, others, such as the Sun Life Insurance Company, with a great deal of publicity. Many Quebecers who were not personally inclined to leave were faced with the choice of a life in Montreal or a job in Toronto. Those who left were, in many cases, leaders in their community and active in their hospitals, churches, and voluntary groups. All of these institutions suffered as a result. The fabric of the English community was weakened, and many feared that it was being destroyed.

Dedicated as it was to the creation of a sort of French-speaking Sweden in America, the Parti Québécois had many priorities in those days. The English community was not one of them. Public declarations by the premier, René Lévesque, and his colleagues were designed to put the English in their place. They were referred to as the "white Rhodesians" of America. Bernard Landry, the minister of state for economic development, said that he was "not sorry that our masters are leaving,"[6] and the premier, in a celebrated statement, declared that the English and French in Quebec were irreconcilable, like two scorpions in a bottle. The government was concentrating all its efforts on the independence referendum, scheduled for 1980, and the English community was rightly considered to be a lost cause so far as this project was concerned.

At the time of the Parti Québécois victory in November 1976, the English community, as such, lacked political leadership. In fact, it was only just becoming aware that it was a Quebec community and that leadership was needed. Its traditional political leaders, federal politicians in Ottawa, were powerless in the face of the new forces at work in Quebec.

The community had really only become fully aware of its provincial representatives for the first time in 1974, during the debate over the Liberal government's language legislation. And having been made aware, it was not impressed. As sponsors of that legislation, the Liberals, especially the three English cabinet ministers, had incurred the wrath of the entire English community and its news media. Faced with the elections of 1976, two of the three, Kevin Drummond in Westmount and William Tetley in Notre-Dame-de-Grâce, were unable even to retain the Liberal nomination in their own constituencies, and both retired from active politics. Victor Goldbloom, the third minister, was re-elected, but his majority was reduced by almost 50 percent.

English voters were furious with the Bourassa government and were seeking any alternative except the one offered by the Parti Québécois. In an effort to restore his credibility in the English community, Bourassa decided to bring in a new face from outside the province (a solution he was to turn to again thirteen years later, when he was faced with a similar crisis[7]). It was announced that Bryce Mackasey, a federal member of Parliament and a former cabinet minister in the Trudeau government, would run in Notre-Dame-de-Grâce and become the new spokesman for English Quebec in a re-elected Liberal government.

On election day, Mackasey won but the Liberals lost. The English community found itself without a single representative in the new Parti Québécois government. The Liberal opposition had only twenty-six members (six of them English-speaking) and no leader. One English Quebecer was elected as a third-party candidate in a protest vote.[8]

The idea that Bryce Mackasey could speak for the English community was conceived in desperation and was unrealistic. His own lack of interest in playing this role was obvious, and within fifteen months he had resigned his seat and returned to Ottawa. A few months later, Victor Goldbloom resigned as well.[9]

Outside the political arena, English leadership was no more evident. There were many prominent English Quebecers—academics, religious leaders, journalists, artists, businesspeople, and professionals—but none of these would have seen themselves as spokespeople for the "community." There were at the time not more than a handful of English Quebecers who would have been able to make their way to Quebec City and present a brief to a legislative commission, an activity in which they were soon to become experts.

In fact, as was frequently pointed out, the English "community" of Quebec was not really aware of its own existence. For French-speaking Quebecers, *les anglais* represented something real, a homogeneous group with a distinct personality. For *les anglais* themselves, there was no collective identity to speak of. They were simply Canadians living in Quebec. The only elements binding them together were the two daily English newspapers in Montreal—the *Gazette* and the *Star*—and their TV and radio stations. The interest groups to which they gave their time and energy reflected a wide range of concerns, but the survival of the English language and its "community" had certainly not been one of them.

With the election of the Parti Québécois, all this changed. The English discovered that they did exist as a group, at least in the minds and the hearts of the French majority. It might be said that the English "community" in Quebec was invented by the French, and the invention was not a pretty thing to see. It was, in many ways, a caricature. Furthermore the English discovered that this distorted image of a community, which they hardly knew existed, but to which they belonged nevertheless, was being used as the basis for some very harsh laws and some even harsher declarations.

One of the things English Quebecers were being told was that they were a minority that had been acting for too long as if it were a majority. A majority is normally unaware of itself as such, and this had been the case with the English. The French in Quebec insisted that the English awaken to their own existence and then transform their understanding of themselves into that of a minority. Reluctantly, the English accepted the invitation, and the "community," as it is known today, was born.

The first signs of life were not in the political arena. Among the thirty or so "patriotic" organizations that sprang up across Canada after the victory of the Parti Québécois were a number in Quebec itself. Among the first of these was Participation Quebec, a group of young Quebecers led by Michael Prupas and Betty Palik, whose efforts were directed at encouraging a greater integration by English Quebecers into the life of the province.

The largest and most visible group, however, was the Positive Action Committee. It was led by Alex Paterson, a Montreal lawyer, and Storrs McCall, a professor of philosophy at McGill University. They formed a group of one hundred English educators, businesspeople, and professionals to publish an open letter to the premier on language policy in April 1977. This initiative inspired the creation of a movement with over fifty thousand English-speaking members. The objective of Positive Action was dialogue and mutual understanding between the two language groups. It presented the most comprehensive brief to the government on behalf of the English community during the debate on Bill 101.

In the following months, a number of other groups appeared and their activities grew in scope as the debate on independence became more intense. Some of these organizations were started outside Montreal, in regions such as the Eastern Townships, Quebec City, Gaspé, and the Outaouais area. In May 1982 an organization incorporating all the members of these bodies, now over twenty in number, was formed as Alliance Quebec. The first president of the Alliance was Eric Maldoff. He and the organization he led were quickly accepted as the official voice of Quebec's English community.

Signs of Hope

In early 1978, the first small sign of hope for the English appeared on the political front. Claude Ryan was elected leader of the Liberal Party of Quebec.

Ryan was the respected editor of *Le Devoir*, a man of stature

26

and independent mind. He had, in fact, supported the Parti Québécois in the 1976 election and had urged his readers to vote against the same Liberal Party that he now proposed to lead. But English Quebecers could identify with his criticisms of the former Bourassa government, and Ryan was now willing to take a stand against a government supported by a movement that seemed invincible and irresistible in its crusade for a new, independent, and French Quebec.

More importantly, Ryan declared his openness to the English community. He liked things to be clear, and as part of his leadership campaign he published a statement on the language question entitled "Declaration of Claude Ryan on Language Policy."[10] In it, he stated his belief that the English community in Quebec had "the right to an open and explicit legal recognition."

- He also promised to eliminate a number of articles in Bill 101, including section 58, which "abusively forbade" the use of English on signs;

- He stated that English schools should be open to all English-speaking children "regardless of their place of birth";

- He promised that the government would deal with English-speaking citizens in their own language;

- He said that health and social services for the English community should be available in English;

- He said that municipalities, if they so desired, should be allowed to function in English as well as French; and

- He promised to dismantle the bureaucratic structures that had been set up to supervise and enforce the application of the Charter of the French Language.

In the context of the times, these proposals seemed to the English community to be a major step in the right direction. The *Montreal Star* declared Ryan to be "a man with a profound sense of justice and a deep concern for the human condition."

It advised its readers that "it was a far cry from the hot gospellers of the Parti Québécois to his position, and for that we should be grateful."[11]

Not all of English Quebec agreed with Claude Ryan. A substantial number of English-speakers felt that *any* restrictive language legislation was unjust. The more passionate and committed of these formed a movement for total "freedom of choice," which was later to become a short-lived political party. But most of the English were ready to follow the emerging leadership of their new community in an effort to work with Ryan and within the Liberal Party. Their objective was to reach a negotiated compromise on language legislation in the hope that the party would someday regain power and implement this new social contract.

This compromise between leaders of the English and French communities in Quebec, within the framework of the Liberal Party, was hammered out over the following eight years. Broadly speaking, it resembled the original propositions in Ryan's declaration of 1978. Its final form can be seen in the resolution on the English community adopted immediately before the elections of 1985, which returned the Liberals to power. This resolution is, to this day, the best summary of the consensus that the English community in Quebec has worked out to ensure its future, at least on matters within the jurisdiction of the provincial government. It reads as follows.

CONSIDERING THAT of all the minority groups in Quebec the English-language community is the largest and the most deeply rooted;

CONSIDERING THAT this community represents one of the two founding peoples of Canada;

CONSIDERING THAT its distinct status should be recognized and that steps should be taken to encourage its full participation in Quebec society;

IT IS RESOLVED THAT:

— A Liberal government will guarantee to the English-language community the right to the orientation and the administration of its educational, cultural, health, and social service institutions;

— A Liberal government will ensure that the services of public and parapublic institutions are available to members of the English community in their own language;

— A Liberal government will undertake to increase the representation of anglophones in the public and parapublic service to a level which reflects the numerical importance of this group;

— A Liberal government will respect the right to post signs in languages other than French, provided the rights of the francophone majority are respected.[12]

This resolution was not pieced together at the last minute. It was the political translation of a consensus reached, after much debate, within the whole community, under the leadership of Alliance Quebec. Every element of it was discussed, approved, and adopted by the party on many occasions. In 1978, during the first by-election after the Parti Québécois victory, Ryan wrote an open letter to the electors of Notre-Dame-de-Grâce in which he recalled the promises of his original declaration.[13] They were repeated by him a few months later in a letter to the English community in his own riding of Argenteuil. They also formed part of the Liberal Party program in 1980 and of the election campaign in 1981. They were still there when Bourassa became leader of the party in 1983, and they were confirmed again in the election campaign of 1985.

It is important to note that the promises in this resolution were not grafted, for electoral purposes, onto a political party whose underlying ideology could not support them. They were rooted in a conception of Quebec society, and of society in general, that was articulated most clearly by a liberal philosophy. While acknowledging the importance of the *collective* rights of the French-

29

speaking majority (and of the English minority as well), the
Liberal position was constructed to a large extent on a notion of
individual rights and liberties that was completely absent from
the rhetoric of the Parti Québécois, which was then in power. It
was, after all, the Liberal Party that had conceived and adopted
the Quebec Charter of Human Rights and Freedoms in 1975 to
protect the citizen from discrimination and guarantee freedom
of expression.

Ryan was an articulate spokesman in attaching his proposals
for the English community to a personal vision of a liberal society
based on the primacy of individual rights. In a memorable speech
in 1978, promising to repeal the signs law, he declared that

> Our concept of democracy . . . has got to be founded on
> the inalienable primacy of individual freedoms. . . . Once
> you have alienated your individual liberties in favour of so-
> called collective rights, they never come back. Collective
> rights become ebonized, they become the norm, they
> become the insurmountable obstacle, and as we can see in
> other countries in the world, once you take that path, it is
> very hard to come back to the norms that you had before.
> So we have a society here based on the primacy of individ-
> ual freedoms. We have been tempted to toy with these
> concepts in the past few years because we thought that
> democracy could be shaken without being put in
> jeopardy. Well, we have got to learn now, we have to realize
> that you cannot play with these fundamental concepts
> irresponsibly. Whatever you do in an irresponsible fash-
> ion you've got to pay for sooner or later. . . . This is our
> concept of democracy, and you can count on me to
> uphold and promote that concept as long as I am leader
> of the Liberal Party.[14]

Ryan's successor understood this as well. Mr. Bourassa, not
normally given to public reflection on abstract principles of
political ideology, stated as recently as 1986 that the government's
intention to permit languages other than French on signs was

"based on values which are profoundly rooted in the liberal tradition. It is not circumstantial or electoralist."[15]

In other words, for ten years, from 1978 to 1988, the English community was given every reason to believe that its traditional home in the Liberal Party of Quebec was safe and that the commitments being made by the French-speaking members of that party were not just an effort at accommodation but a genuine article of faith, a reflection of the way they saw the world. The English were encouraged by their leaders to believe that it was only necessary to work with the Liberals and that the new social contract would follow naturally after their election victory.

Leadership

Political compromise does not materialize from the atmosphere. It is the result of negotiations between individuals who wish to get along with each other. The English community was represented during this period by a remarkable number of individuals who emerged from the newly created "community" to take a full role in Quebec life. At the political level, three new members of the National Assembly—Richard French, Clifford Lincoln, and Herbert Marx, all of whom became ministers in the Bourassa government—played an important role. Each, in his own way, articulated the views of the English community.

Even more important were the leaders of community organizations, both the traditional ones, such as the school and hospital boards, and the new, more broadly based institutions under the umbrella of Alliance Quebec. Among the most visible of these leaders were Eric Maldoff, Alex Paterson, Michael Goldbloom, Charles Taylor, Storrs McCall, Robert Keaton, Michael Prupas, Dr. Jim Ross, Royal Orr, Joan Dougherty, Anne Usher, John Simms, Bob Dobie, and Geoffrey Chambers. There were many more. All were supported by an impressive number of concerned Quebecers who worked at every level in the community organiza-

31

tions and who supported, both privately and publicly, the search for accommodation and consensus.

The search for a reasonable compromise was not easy. General opinion in the English community was always less inclined to moderation than was its leadership. The executive of Alliance Quebec often met resistance from its large board of directors, and the board itself was more inclined to compromise than were the members it represented. But those most closely involved in the discussions with the leaders of the French community knew that there were fundamentalists on both sides and that the final arrangements would necessarily be in the form of a compromise.

Within the Liberal Party there were French-speaking leaders who encouraged and took part in the creation of this compromise. Among the elected members there was Ryan himself, and later, Bourassa. Both of the other candidates for the leadership of the Liberal Party in 1983, Daniel Johnson and Pierre Paradis, confirmed their commitment to the program. Within the party two successive presidents, Louise Robic and Robert Benoit, publicly confirmed their approval of the consensus as well. Together, in private conversations, workshops, committee meetings, and finally in Liberal Party conferences, a definition of the future status of the English community, satisfactory to all, was worked out, and, in the process, both sides got to know each other better.

What has been briefly recalled above is a decade of effort by a few dozen leaders of the English-speaking community, supported, at times hesitantly, by its members, to reach a compromise with their French-speaking neighbours on their role and status in modern Quebec society. That consensus was worked out and approved within the framework of the Liberal Party of Quebec. It was not a last-minute addition to that party's program, but the result of ten years of negotiations within a party whose fundamental ideology was totally consistent with the consensus reached.

To arrive at this consensus, English Quebecers had been obliged to transform their perception of themselves in less than a decade. In the eyes of the French majority, the English-speaking community had existed for generations. Now, for the first time, the English came to understand this definition of themselves. Accepting it, they agreed to work, as a minority, within the political and social structures of Quebec. They accepted the need to protect the French language in Quebec against erosion. In return, their own community structures would be secured and strengthened by a series of specific guarantees, five in number, to be adopted and implemented by a Liberal government.

THE SIGNS DEBATE OF 1988

What treasure, uncle?
Tennis-balls, my liege.

Henry V
Act I, scene ii

The Background

In December 1985, the resurrected Liberal government of Robert Bourassa was elected with 97 seats out of 122 and with the overwhelming support of the English population. The long wait was over. The Liberal "consensus" on the English community, worked out over ten years, could now be realized.

But it was not to be. Three years later, practically none of the commitments had been respected, the leadership of the English community had been seriously undermined, and the consensus arrived at was being openly abandoned by the French-speaking majority. The event that became the focal point of this repudiation was the government's decision to forbid the use of English-language signs.

Seen from outside Quebec, the debate about the language of commercial signs is incredible. Robert Bourassa himself has pointed out that "nowhere in the free world is there a country where the minority is prohibited from using its own language on its signs."[16]

But from the earliest days of language legislation in Quebec, one element considered essential was to make the "visible face" of Quebec appear more French. The original idea was not to forbid the use of other languages, but to ensure that the language of the majority was not neglected. Many large merchants were English-speaking, and for years they had failed to show sufficient respect for their French-speaking clientele to inform them in their own language. Most French-speaking consumers, in turn, had not been sufficiently upset to force the issue by insisting on their own language or shopping elsewhere. In Montreal and Quebec City, English-language signs were widely used because of the large transient clientele, many of whom were English. Furthermore, many French merchants used English signs because that language was considered to be more universally understood.

The Gendron Report of 1972 had not considered the question of the language of signs to be central to the future of the French language. It had simply recommended that "in the public and parapublic sectors, the use of French be obligatory" and that no other language "take precedence over the French inscription."[17] Bill 22, the Liberal Party's 1974 language legislation, carried this principle of compulsory French, with no prohibition on other languages, into the private sector as well, stating that all public signs "must be drawn up in French or in both French and another language."

After 1976, however, the newly elected Parti Québécois government decided that the presence of *any* English on signs, particularly in Montreal, would send a message to French-speaking Quebecers that they could communicate in either English *or* French. It was also claimed that immigrants to Quebec who spoke neither language would interpret English on signs as a signal that they could be served, work, and live in that language.

These claims were never supported by anything resembling a logical argument. Even if one accepted the premise that people should be discouraged from communicating in English in Quebec, no empirical evidence was ever presented to indicate that the language of signs would be a factor in such a decision. Nor has there been any since. In fact, the presence of English on signs has been a fact of life in Quebec for over two hundred years, during which the use of French has continued to expand. The idea that it had to be eliminated became, simply, a fetish.

In any event, with the adoption of Bill 101, the law was amended to state that "public signs and posters and commercial advertising shall be *solely* in the official language."[18] As a result, on August 26, 1977, it became illegal (with a few exceptions) to post new signs carrying English words anywhere in Quebec. Most of the existing English-language signs were to be replaced within one year. So, in 1978, thousands of signs all over Quebec, especially in Montreal, were prohibited and a supervisory commission was established to see that they were taken down and replaced. The objective was no longer to ensure the use of French. It was to create the facade of a totally French community, on the premise that the reflection might eventually transform the reality.

Most of the other sections of the Charter of the French Language related to activities in the *public* sector. The signs legislation, however, was an intrusion into the *private* sector, and as a result the opposition to it was particularly vehement.

As might be expected the law was contested in the courts, on the grounds that it violated both Quebec's and Canada's charters of human rights and freedoms, which guarantee each citizen freedom of expression and freedom from discrimination based on language. In December 1984,[19] the Quebec Superior Court agreed that there was such a violation and declared the sign laws to be invalid. It ruled that laws could be adopted to require the use of French on signs, but not to forbid other languages. The Parti Québécois government immediately launched an appeal to a higher court, and a year later, in 1985, when the Liberals were elected to power, the decision on this appeal was still pending.

True to its election promises, the new Liberal government confirmed its intention to change the law and permit bilingual signs. But it announced that it would wait for the decision of the Court of Appeal before acting. It expected to obtain further vindication for its position from that decision. It also wished to ensure that the new rules to be established would conform to the court's definition of the point at which individual and collective rights intersect in such an issue.

This decision did not unduly concern the English community. The debate had already been carried out within the Liberal Party, and the issue had been settled. The new government was committed to bilingual signs. It was delaying implementation simply to permit a more orderly transition, on the basis of what everyone expected to be a confirmation of the first ruling.

The premier continued to be unequivocal in his commitment to the change. In the autumn of 1986 he stated, "It is certainly for me a profound conviction . . . that it is a question of common sense to not forbid or prohibit the use of other languages."[20] He even suggested that the regulations might be changed to permit bilingual signs, without changing the law itself.[21] To make his intentions perfectly clear, on October 21, 1986, with the court's decision imminent, the government created a task force to advise it on ways in which the necessary changes could be translated into legislation. The task force's report was submitted on December 19 of the same year.[22]

The Crisis

Three days later, on December 22, 1986, the Quebec Court of Appeal unanimously declared that the signs law violated fundamental human rights and was invalid. But then, to the consternation of the English community, a surprising thing happened. The government did not act as it had promised. Instead, it decided to appeal the decision again, this time to the Supreme Court of Canada.[23]

With the benefit of hindsight, one can see that any changes to the signs legislation were probably doomed from that day onward. The reasons given for appealing the case were technical, and in justifying them the minister of justice, Herbert Marx, said that they in no way prevented the government from permitting bilingual signs at once, if it wanted to.[24]

But from this moment the government's commitment to make the change became much more equivocal. The Liberal Party adopted a resolution at its general council meeting that approved the appeal and urged the government to strengthen its efforts to enforce the existing law until the decision was rendered.

Two years elapsed before the Supreme Court of Canada handed down the final decision on the signs issue. During that period the forces opposed to any English on signs—in the community, in the Parti Québécois opposition, and in the Liberal Party and the caucus—mounted a campaign of steadily increasing intensity.

The premier and the ministers directly concerned left these

forces all the space they required. They refused to comment on the issue, on the grounds that the matter was before the courts and that their silence was in the interests of "social peace."[25] The premier implied, in effect, that he would not respect the court's decision if those opposed to it created a disturbance. The announcement was an invitation to agitation that proved impossible to resist.

As a result of all this, when the Supreme Court decision was finally made public on December 15, 1988,[26] language tensions in Quebec had reached a level reminiscent of 1976. Groups opposed to bilingual signs were protesting the decision in the streets a few hours after it was handed down.

They had reason to protest. The Supreme Court unanimously confirmed the decisions of the two lower courts. It too declared that the prohibition of English on signs violated both the Quebec and Canadian charters of human rights, and that it was a limitation on freedom of expression and a form of discrimination based on language.

The Quebec government quickly decided that it would not accept this decision. Within three days the premier announced he would invoke a clause of the Canadian constitution that permits governments to adopt laws, notwithstanding their infringement of the federal Charter, for a renewable period of five years.[27] The government would amend the signs legislation to permit some English on signs inside a store, but none outside.

Faced with immediate objections to even this concession, the new legislation was quickly changed, before its adoption, to prohibit all except the smallest shops in Quebec from using any language except French anywhere on their premises, inside or outside.[28] A few days later the premier declared that the new sign law "barely changes" the existing law, and that "when perception catches up with reality, Quebecers will finally notice that we are maintaining unilingual French everywhere, inside and outside."[29]

This "reality" was quickly apparent to the members of Bourassa's government. On December 20, three of his most senior English-speaking ministers resigned. Richard French, minister of communications; Clifford Lincoln, minister of the environment; and Herbert Marx, minister of public security, expressed essentially the same opinion in announcing their intention to leave the government in which they were key figures. They fully accepted the need to ensure the presence of French on signs, but they could not live with the exclusion of other languages.

Herbert Marx stated that he had "always been against the suspension of fundamental liberties with a 'notwithstanding clause'," that it was "a question of conscience, a question of principle."[30] Richard French maintained that "the cultural rights of one group cannot result in the negation of the cultural rights of others."[31]

Clifford Lincoln argued that "whoever tampers with a very delicate machinery of equity and justice in a society, which are expressed through rights, sets in motion a change of events which someone more audacious may tamper with even more."[32] The rhetoric unleashed throughout Canada during the debate over the Meech Lake constitutional amendments that followed,[33] and the breakdown of that agreement, suggest that Lincoln was not overstating his case.

The adoption of Bill 178, the law forbidding the use of English signs, took place before the Christmas recess in 1988. Every French-speaking Liberal member of the National Assembly voted for it, including those who had been most involved, over the previous ten years, in building the Liberal Party program for the English community.

As might be expected, Alliance Quebec, the community's nonpolitical voice and a principal architect of the program, did not emerge unscathed. It was caught in the crossfire of the recriminations that ensued, and within a few weeks its president, Royal Orr, had resigned.[34]

In effect, relations between the English and French communities were set back to about where they were in 1976. The minority community once again found itself without leadership, a sense of its place in the larger Quebec society, or a political party with which it could identify.

How the French Community Reacted

It was to be expected that the English community would be outraged by Bill 178, and it was. But what about the French community? It had, after all, been part of the agreement, explicitly in the development of the Liberal Party program and implicitly in voting massively for that party in 1985. It might be assumed that the French community also felt some attachment in this matter to the Quebec Charter of Human Rights and Freedoms, which the signs law had clearly violated. Not so. It soon became clear that in his effort to respond to the mood of the moment, the premier had hit the nail directly on the head.

Inevitably the Parti Québécois and its traditional clientele argued that the law did not go far enough and that English should be forbidden on all signs, everywhere. But at that time they represented only a small minority. Virtually the entire French-speaking population, on which the Liberal Party depended for its own re-election, fully supported Bill 178 or remained silent on the issue. Claude Ryan, the father of the original agreement with the English community and then minister of education, explained his reversal by announcing his recent discovery of a "profound attachment of Quebec's francophones for Bill 101, and the identification which had been created in the minds of the population between that law and the defence of the French language."[35] Furthermore, he announced that he did not agree with the Supreme Court that the right to one's choice of language in commercial matters was a question of fundamental rights.[36]

The Liberal Party, convened in special session two days after the Supreme Court decision, adopted a resolution, proposed by its president, that only French should be permitted on external signs.[37] In the course of a few hours, the results of ten years of negotiation between the English and French within the party were, to put it politely, abandoned.

In the larger community, very few French-speaking Quebecers permitted themselves to be tortured by the ruling of the Supreme Court that Bill 178 was a clear violation of human rights. Lysiane Gagnon, one of the most widely-read columnists in Quebec, noted that three of the five Supreme Court judges who rendered the decision were English and argued that things might have been different if more French judges had been involved.[38]

Other leaders of French opinion followed Ryan in arguing that signs were "commercial" and that freedom of expression did not, or should not, apply to this kind of activity.[39] The court had specifically addressed this issue in its decision by stating that "commercial expression, like political expression, is one of the forms of expression that is deserving of constitutional protection because it serves individual and societal values in a free and democratic society."

The most important evidence that the government had "got it right" politically was the reaction of the French-speaking business community. Within hours of the decision, the two main employer groups in Quebec, the Chamber of Commerce and the Conseil de Patronat, had announced their support for the law.[40] Not one business leader spoke a single word in public against the decision. The powerful French-speaking business community was a vital ally of the Liberal government. Its support was essential, and it gave it.

Furthermore, with only one exception, not a single French-speaking public figure in Quebec expressed support for the position of the English community. The iconoclast was Benoit Lauzière, director of *Le Devoir,* who in his editorial on the subject asked, "Will the presence of other marks on a face that is clearly French be a denial of what we really are, or in fact a better expression of it?" He concluded, "French everywhere, yes, but not at the price of a censorship of liberty of expression which prevents someone else from being visible."[41]

But Lauzière stood alone and was publicly criticized by his own colleagues for the position he took.[42] When the dust had settled, Premier Bourassa was able to take satisfaction from the expression of public opinion that counts most. The first poll of voting intentions taken after the decision (in January 1989)[43] revealed that 56 percent of the population would still support the Liberal Party if an election were to be held at that time.

The French-speaking community in Quebec had been satisfied that the Liberal Party was, at last, the committed defender of the French language, that it had finally learned to say "no" to the English. Any lingering doubts about the human-rights aspect were dispelled by assurances that the Supreme Court ruling had been a decision by "English judges" on a minor aspect of the human-rights issue that should probably not even have been considered as such at all. A clear statement had been made that "Quebec is French." And the French of Quebec were not displeased.

The Other Commitments of the Liberal Party

The right to English-language signs was the most spectacular of the promises made to the English community by the Liberal Party, but it was not the only one and perhaps not the most important. A fair evaluation of the government's respect for its commitment requires a consideration, as well, of its other four promises:

— formal recognition of the English community's distinct status in Quebec society.

— the right to the orientation and administration of its own educational, cultural, health, and social service institutions.

— an increase in the representation of English-speaking Quebecers in the public and parapublic sectors to reflect that community's numerical importance.

— the extension of government services in the English language.

44

Distinct Status

This element of the program faithfully reflects Claude Ryan's declaration in 1978 that the English-language community in Quebec has "the right to an open and explicit legal recognition." Nothing has been done by the Liberal government to make this recognition more explicit than it was in 1985. The subject has not even been raised inside Quebec.

The government did commit itself to the principle, in a way, with the Meech Lake constitutional agreement,[44] in which it was stated that English-speaking Canadians "present in Quebec" constitute a fundamental characteristic of the country and that the provincial legislature of Quebec has a role in "preserving" it.

But the Meech Lake agreement had no connection with the Liberal Party program for the English. It was never understood that the recognition of this distinct status for English Quebecers would be conditional on a constitutional amendment, or that the English of Quebec could be used as hostages in a federal–provincial debate. The commitment in the Liberal program was an agreement within the Quebec community about the relations that should exist between groups *within* our society.

Neither before nor after the Meech Lake debate has any effort been made by Quebec's Liberal government to give a meaning to this distinct status. Is it the same as the distinct status claimed by the government of Quebec in the Canadian federation? The English of Quebec have come to think of themselves as a "community," while the French tend to refer to themselves as a "society." The two words do not mean exactly the same thing, but in view of the semantic free-for-all that generally prevails in the world of politics (and even among those who draft constitutions), it is not unreasonable to assume that the rights and protections that might be claimed by a distinct "community" would not be very different from, and certainly not fewer than, those claimed by a distinct "society." In any event, the discussion on this matter has not even begun.

As a result, the "open and explicit legal recognition" of the English minority in Quebec that was proposed by Ryan and promised by Bourassa has not come to pass. The existing fragmentary constitutional and legal protections are found only in the Canadian constitution, and they were there long before 1985. Nothing has been done since then to clarify and give some strength to the commitment.

Institutions

The maintenance of publicly supported educational and health and social service institutions is the most important single gesture the state can make to recognize a linguistic community. It is also very difficult; it requires both a political commitment and the allocation of scarce resources. The government wishes to avoid expensive duplications in the system, some of which are inevitable with parallel institutions. It wishes to ensure uniform "national" standards of education and health care, a difficult task in a system that includes autonomous boards and commissions.

In Quebec, English institutions exist in the educational and health sectors because the English community developed them long before the state concerned itself with these matters and, in the case of Protestant education, because of constitutional guarantees that were given in 1867.

The concerns of the English community are that the character of these distinctive institutions is being progressively weakened by the administrative and financial constraints of the public sector and by lack of interest in maintaining a viable English alternative. As a result, the Liberals promised to guarantee the English the right to determine "the orientation and the administration" of their own institutions. With one exception, this promise has not been respected since the Liberals took power.

EDUCATION In the educational sector, the distinct structures already exist in the form of school boards and the governing

46

councils in the colleges and universities. There is a separate English educational system within the confessional structures guaranteed in the constitution. The limitations on it are in the form of access to the schools and control over their curriculum, and in the case of the universities, funding.

Access to schools is limited by a requirement that all students who are not English-speaking should use the French school system. This rule, which was at the heart of the language debate in the early 1960s, is now widely, if not universally, accepted. However, access to English schools is also denied to English-speaking students as well, unless their parents were educated in English *in Canada*. The obvious limitation this places on the movement of people from other countries, notably the United States, has been reduced only slightly by a cumbersome and discriminatory system of "temporary" permits. Furthermore, the minister of education has stated that his government now wishes to "re-examine" even the existing constitutional right of English Canadians to send their children to English schools.[45]

The school curriculum for both English and French schools is established in Quebec City by a bureaucracy that is, to all intents, totally French-speaking, and a uniform "national" program has been developed. Not only has the government refused to allow greater freedom over the curriculum to the English sector, it has argued in the Supreme Court that, while the English should be allowed to participate in the management of their educational facilities, they should *not* have the right to control them.[46] It is impossible to reconcile this position with one that guarantees the English community the right to the "orientation and administration" of its own system.

At the university level, all three of Quebec's English-speaking institutions are underfunded by the government, in comparison with their French-language equivalents. The minister of education has acknowledged this since 1985 but has refused to re-establish parity, stating that the government will not be bound by "blind arithmetic" in allocating funds.[47]

HEALTH CARE In the health care and social service systems there is no legally recognized distinct English sector, as there is in the educational system, although a number of hospitals and homes are English by tradition. The government has given no indication that it is prepared to establish such a distinct network.

However, in 1986, in response to an election promise, the government adopted legislation intended to increase the availability of English-language services in existing institutions.[48] Since then some genuine efforts have been made to put the wheels of reform in motion. But no one has been arrested for speeding in the implementation of this law. Five years after its adoption, approximately 40 percent of the funds promised had been committed to the project.

Services in English

The provision of services to the English-speaking citizen requires the production of forms, brochures, and documents in English and their distribution to the places where they are needed. It requires staff—in Quebec City, in the regional offices of the government, and on its boards and commissions—who are able to speak and write in English.

In most ministries it is still difficult to obtain either written or oral information in English. With a few exceptions, there is no obligation placed on the numerous departments of government ministries and boards to provide these services. The English services that do exist were available when the Liberal government took power in 1985. Since then, no action has been taken to provide a greater level of service, to propose a policy for the future, or even to establish an inventory of the services available in the English language at present.

Representation in the Public Sector

The government has not respected its commitment to increase English representation in the civil service to "a level which respects the numerical importance of this group." In fact, members of the English community in Quebec make up less than 1 percent of its public service, even though they constitute more than 10 percent of the population. This figure appears to have decreased since the Liberal Party took power in 1985.[49] At the senior levels of government, only three of the 165 provincial deputy ministers are English.[50]

Another example of the government's unwillingness to act can be seen in the many public and parapublic institutions that administer the delivery of countless services to the community, from the protection of human rights to the regulation of professional services. The administrators of these bodies are appointed by the government in a process closely controlled by the premier's office. The English community's presence in them is so small as to be almost invisible. At present, only five of these 162 organizations have an English Quebecer as chairperson.[51]

Premier Bourassa has stated that he has no intention of correcting this situation. In his 1989 election campaign he committed himself, "over time," to increase the representation of all minority groups in the civil service *except the English,* who, he argued, have other ways of making their views known.[52]

The conclusion is inescapable. The "English agenda" of the Liberal Party, to which it committed itself in the 1985 election, has not been respected. With the single exception of the law to provide health services in English, it has been either neglected (as in the case of English representation in the civil service), or explicitly contradicted (as in the case of the signs law).

Why the Liberals' Promises Were Not Kept

So far this book has been recounting a story, and it would be helpful to recognize it as the story of a failure. The English community set out to do something and they did not get it done, after working at it for over ten years.

Assuming that as victims of this experience, we do not wish to relive it, it might be useful to understand how it all came to pass—how it happened that only a few months after the election of the Liberal government in 1985, its commitments to the English community were relegated to the time-honoured and abundant repository of unfulfilled election promises.

The events that signalled this change in direction came about mainly because of the acute sensitivity of the government to any issue that touches on language. This preoccupation was severely tested by public reaction to three events that occurred in the early months of the new Liberal mandate. Two of these had nothing to do with the government's promises to the English community.

A few months after the election in 1985, the Liberal government found itself obliged to grant an amnesty to a number of students whose parents had not respected the retroactive clauses in the 1977 Charter of the French Language and had illegally kept their children in the English school system. This was seized upon by the nationalist opposition as an opportunity to demonstrate that the Liberal government was not interested in protect-- ing the French language.[53]

The second event occurred only a few weeks later, when the government announced, for reasons never made clear, its intention to reorganize and "rationalize" the various bodies that administer the language laws.[54] This time the protests of the nationalist element were even stronger, and they were on stronger ground. The project, as presented, was difficult to justify or even to explain. The government withdrew the legislation, and nothing more was ever heard of it.

Soon thereafter, the government introduced its promised legislation to guarantee English services in the health system.[55] By this time, the regular attacks on the Liberals' excessive preoccupation with the English had made the government so nervous that the bill was fiercely opposed by many inside the Liberal caucus itself, and it was considerably diluted in its effect before adoption.

From that moment onward, the Liberal government, under pressure from both its caucus and media opinion, decided that its efforts to satisfy the English community were over. The time had come, in its view, to be seen as the defender of the language of the majority. The government's December 1988 decision to forbid the use of English on signs was, in effect, the logical extension of a new attitude toward the English that had evolved during the previous three years. An understanding of the reasons for this change is essential in determining a strategy for the English of Quebec in the years that lie ahead.

The first thing to note is that during this period the French-speaking leadership in Quebec, which had insisted that the English community begin to think of itself as a minority, neglected to explain the consequences of this to their own people. If the English were to see themselves in that way, then the French would be obliged to behave as a majority. Unfortunately, they did not. In fact, the very opposite perception was openly encouraged—and still is—with the result that French-speaking Quebecers continue to think of their community as a minority group as well, weaker and more threatened than ever. In such a climate of mutual insecurity, the possibility for reconciliation and accommodation is practically impossible.

There are two conditions that together have created this situation. The first is fact: the French language is spoken by only a tiny minority of the people in North America. The presence and the attraction of English as an alternative to French is evident to every worker, to every mother and father.

But this situation does not mean that a feeling of insecurity is inevitable. These constraints have existed since 1759, and there are all kinds of indications that the French-speaking community in Quebec has never been stronger than it is today. Nearly 83 percent of the population is French-speaking, up from 80 percent a decade ago, and the English community has suffered a corresponding decline in that period. In Montreal, where assimilation in English is most feared, everyone agrees that the use of French is more widespread than ever before. The majority of the English community speaks French, which has become the "common language" of the whole community. The frequently remarked arrival of a French-speaking elite in the business sector is a fact, and there is no longer any significant gap between the average incomes of the two language groups.

One might imagine that, under such conditions, the leaders of the French-speaking community would have attempted to instil their fellow citizens with confidence in themselves and tell them that they are strong, on the well-founded conviction that those who possess such confidence are likely to become even more successful.

Not so. The recurring theme of the intellectual and political leaders of Quebec is that the French community and its language are weaker and in greater danger than ever before. In some cases, this attitude is the honest conclusion to an attempt at long-term demographic forecasting. But there are other factors at play as well.

Underlying every effort at reconciliation between the English and the French is a struggle for power in which there are inevitably winners and losers. In Quebec there are actors on the political scene who, for their own reasons, see no advantage in a strong English community in Quebec. The obvious examples are separatist and nationalist organizations, whose objectives can only be made more difficult by a strong English presence. It is in their interest to advise French Quebecers that the English community is still taking up space (even with only 10 percent of the population) that should rightfully be theirs. The unilingual state sought by Lord Durham in 1839[56] is now the goal of others, but on behalf of a different language.

As a result, we are faced with a situation in which there are two groups that believe themselves to be fragile and threatened minorities—in the same political space. If one believes the arguments of both sides, then the English community will no longer exist in Quebec in a few years and everyone who remains will be speaking English!

It is also useful to remember that the issue here, beyond its political dimension, is also a debate between the English and the French. These are two powerful linguistic groups, with different personalities. Their view of each other was formed and nourished in Europe, where the channel that divides England from France is more than sea water. In Canada, the challenge for these two groups, living together in one political space, is to reconcile two personalities that have much in common but see each other as rivals at home and in the world. While the special advantage of life in Quebec is the coexistence of these two great cultures, behind all the rhetoric about who is weak and who is strong there is an inevitable struggle for power between two languages and traditions.

A second factor should be kept in mind to understand why the "English agenda" was abandoned by the Liberal government. A little political history is required to explain it. During the period of Parti Québécois government from 1976 to 1985, the Liberal Party, in opposition, was perceived by many Quebecers as the party of "the English," and in a limited sense this was true. In the 1976 elections the Liberals elected only twenty-six members to the National Assembly, and six of them were English. Another five represented counties in which the majority of the population was not French-speaking, and all but seven of the twenty-six ridings contained substantial language minorities.[57]

As a result, from 1977 to 1981 the strong influence of the English and other non-French-language groups on the party was felt in the National Assembly and in the party's councils and policy-making bodies. Consequently, the Liberals went into the 1981 elections identified by many as the party of "everyone but the French-speaking majority." Their defeat was partly due to that perception.

Immediately after the election the defeated leader, Claude Ryan, began to take a more "nationalistic" posture.[58] It was, however, not sufficient to prevent him from being invited to resign, and he did. But the message was clear to the party executive. When the new leader, Robert Bourassa, created his policy committee to prepare a new political program in 1983, he named only one English-speaking member in a group of thirty-six.[59] It was not surprising that this program, "Maitrisons L'Avenir," made no mention at all of the English community. It was only when this "oversight" was pointed out forcefully in the English press[60] that Bourassa agreed to allow the reinsertion of the English community's traditional concerns into the Liberal Party program.

Then came the election. In the 1981 vote the Liberals had won forty-two seats, thirty of them in constituencies with a strong non-French component.[61] After the 1985 election, there were still thirty "English" Liberal ridings, but out of a total of 99. The influence of the English community in the power structure of the party and the government was reduced overnight by half.

As a result, the Liberal party changed profoundly after the December 1985 election. The promises and the rhetoric that had assured the transfer of fifty-seven additional counties to the Liberal side and made the election victory possible had not dwelt on the role of the English in Quebec. The new members had defeated their Parti Québécois opponents, in part, by assuring the voters that they were *not* "the party of the English." Now in power, they were determined to make this assurance a reality.

The leadership of the party and the government was extremely sensitive to this new nationalist element. For one thing, it was evident that the only political threat to the government was the Parti Québécois. Consequently there was every reason to adopt a political stance that would ensure that only those unequivocally committed to independence would find it necessary to vote for that opposition party. The Liberal Party decided to make certain that all French Canadian nationalists could feel at home within its ranks. To achieve this the English-speaking wing of the party was to be asked to make, in the words of the premier, an "enormous concession."[62]

In retrospect it seems evident that for a broadly based party whose principles are centred, not on an ideology but on gaining and retaining power, the influence that the English were able to exercise within the Liberal Party of Quebec from 1976 to 1983 was unsustainable. The fifty or so new seats won for the Liberals in 1985 and retained in 1989 were exclusively in areas where the population is overwhelmingly French-speaking, and in most cases rural. Control of the party has passed into another orbit.

Finally, in examining the reasons for the repudiation of the English program it is important to note that the present government of Quebec is extremely sensitive to polls and pressure groups. Most issues are considered not on their intrinsic merits, but on the basis of who is for and who is against, and who will make the better ally. There are few programs, few agendas, that will not be amended or cancelled if they are not in harmony with the mood of the moment. Although all governments are sensitive to short-term public opinion, the present Quebec government is supersensitive.

Unfortunately, of all public policy issues language questions are among the most difficult to understand by reading polls. Such statistics are a hopeless effort to establish a scientific basis for what is really a jumble of emotions. A minor change in a question about a language issue will elicit a wholly disproportionate change in the answer given.

As a result, in the language debate, polls can be used to justify almost any course of action. For example, a study made by the polling organization Sorécom of nine major opinion polls on signs between 1979 and 1986 indicated that 50 percent of the French-speaking population want signs in Quebec to be in French only—and 70 percent want them to be bilingual![63]

The most striking example of this contradiction and the intense preoccupation of the government with surveys can been seen in the explanation Premier Bourassa gave for his decision to adopt Bill 178. When asked by the *Financial Times* to explain the reasons for this decision, he replied:

> Opinion polls then were showing that the great majority of French-speaking Quebecers were favouring bilingualism. But they were also showing that a great majority of

Quebecers were unwilling to touch Bill 101, which forbids bilingual signs. You're premier of Quebec and you have two polls, one saying don't touch Bill 101, another poll saying we agree with bilingual signs. What do you do with that? You come up with inside–outside.[64]

This is how the premier resolved the issue of "high principle" for which three English-speaking cabinet ministers gave up their political careers.

The conclusion to all of this is that implementation of the political program developed by and for the English community is impossible, both now and for the foreseeable future. Despite considerable effort, the English community has been unable to create a sustainable consensus in favour of it among the French-speaking majority. A Liberal government will not implement it, regardless of any previous commitment, because the influence of the English in that party has diminished and because the Liberal government will not get in front of its French-speaking clientele on the language issue.

For English Quebecers, the situation is not unlike the one facing French Quebecers after the failure of the Meech Lake constitutional pact. In both cases there was an agreement, consisting of five points, that one of the contracting parties failed to respect. Both agreements had a "distinct society" clause as their centrepiece, and each involved "spending powers" as well. It would be surprising if the two victims did not react in similar ways to the situation in which they find themselves. For the English in Quebec, as for Quebec in Canada, a new way must be found to secure our future.

THE ENGLISH OF QUEBEC

What is my nation?
Who talks of my nation?

Henry V
Act III, scene ii

A Personal Narrative

I grew up in Quebec—or, to be more precise, in the Eastern Townships—and I grew up in English. What was important for me then was my family; my home town, East Angus; and the nearby villages of my grandparents. We had a farm. We made hay there, picked chokecherries, swam, cut wood, shovelled snow.

There was a paper mill in East Angus, with a famous smell that was the town's trademark for miles around. I remember the sound of the logs going into the barking drums; you could hear it for miles on those cold, clear nights of winter. And I remember my grandparents, on my father's side in Bishopton, where I helped sort the mail in their post office, and on my mother's side in North Hatley, where I helped deliver the milk from their farm. I mention this—and there is much more—as a way of saying that my home was, still is, and will remain Quebec.

This was Canada, too. I remember lying in bed early in the morning, listening to the radio, and hearing news about the Canadian soldiers in Europe. But Canada seemed almost to be a part of that Europe, rather than being a part of my life. If there was a world outside my village, it was Quebec. My father talked about Quebec, not Canadian, politics, and the train that went through East Angus carried, in its parlour cars, those wildly important Quebec politicians on their way to the capital.

It seemed quite natural that my father should one day suggest that I learn French. He persuaded me to go for the summer to live with a French family in St-Georges-de-Beauce, a few miles away. After that I went to Bishop's University, also in Quebec. I played on the hockey team, at night, "under the lights," against teams in towns that have names like Coaticook, Sawyerville, and Marbleton.

I could go on; each memory conjures up another. But perhaps this is enough to make the point that my credentials as a native Quebecer are as authentic as those of any of my contemporaries who grew up in French in those very same villages and towns, or in any other part of Quebec.

My story is far from unique. Hundreds of thousands of English Quebecers have memories like this, from the country and from the city, and for them Quebec will always be their home.

Let me say again that this Quebec was for me an English Quebec, even after I learned to speak French. I was fully aware that there were the two groups, and I knew, from my own experience, of injustices (and acts of generosity) by the English and the French toward each other. But none of them altered my belief that I had the right to be English in Quebec.

As a member of the English community in the Eastern Townships, I was not living as a conqueror of the French. The area's first white settlers were my own ancestors. They were English speaking, and the names of the counties and towns left no doubt about this fact. Our religion was mainly Protestant, and our roots were much closer to those of our neighbours in Vermont and New Hampshire than they were to the people of Charlevoix county. We had been caught up within the boundaries of a place called Quebec, and we were English.

Recalling these experiences does not make me nostalgic. I have no desire to relive them. With the rest of our society, I have moved on and I don't want to go back. But I would like to build on what I was given.

As my life continued, I worked in both languages. My company, Perkins Papers, became les Papiers Perkins before any laws required it. In the factories we worked mostly in French, because most of the people spoke that language. The sales department was mostly English, because it sold our products across Canada, but the Quebec division was mainly French. It all seemed so simple at the time.

Later I worked for the Quebec government, mostly in French. Then I went to Ottawa for three years, where the work was done in English and French, and then into politics in Quebec—

French—and then to London, as *délégue générale* of the Quebec office, where it was French in the office and English in the street.

I talk to people in whatever language seems easier for them. It doesn't bother me if they speak only French, or only English. Perhaps learning another language is not one of their priorities; so be it.

For me, Quebec has two languages, French and English. I see no reason why it shouldn't continue to be that way, and many reasons why it can and should. The government should serve its citizens in at least these two languages. The Quebec that we know today was founded as a part of Canada on that premise, and Quebecers signed that agreement. Neither English nor French has become obsolete or irrelevant since that time.

Furthermore, I believe that governments exist to serve individuals—*people*—not some linguistic, religious, or cultural vision. Experience has shown us that usually when governments allow themselves to get carried away by one of the national causes proposed by certain members of their society, *they get it wrong*, frequently with disastrous results for all concerned—including, over time, the intended beneficiaries of the project.

Even a cursory examination of Quebec's history reveals that tensions between English and French have always existed; they are part of the definition of our society. The search for mutual accommodation, with respect for the other's point of view, is well worth the effort. It has a significance that goes beyond the province's borders. It is part of the worldwide challenge that faces people who are different from each other but who must live together in a common humanity.

But the present climate in Quebec does not permit this. What should legitimately be one of a number of the state's preoccupations has become an obsession that colours every political discussion and gesture. Newspapers can move a story from page five to page one if they find a way to give it a linguistic angle. There appears to be no group of people, in the developed world at least, carrying linguistic nationalism to the extremes that exist today in the province of Quebec.

Some say that this is all leading inexorably to political independence. Independence is not inevitable; the country has been through this kind of crisis before. But even if Quebec were to become an independent country, English Quebecers and their language would still be a part of the place. With independence or without it, Quebec will still have to come to terms with the English language. The challenge for all of us is to make this happen in a way that does not divide our society but strengthens it.

Who Are the English?

The preceding personal narrative reflects the experiences and impressions of one English-speaking Quebecer. But there are many English Quebecers, and each one has its own story.

Who are the members of this newly created "community" of individuals who have been here for three hundred years? A number of excellent books and countless documents[65] recount their history. It is clear that they have made a tremendous contribution to the political, economic, cultural, and social edifice that is the province of Quebec.

Today they number about 700,000. Like French Quebecers, they are immigrants, or descendants of immigrants, to the New World. The largest single group is Anglo-Saxon, from the British Isles, and it is this group that provides raw material for the caricature of the whole community that has become established in the public mind. But Anglo-Saxons make up less than 60 percent of the community, and this percentage is dropping steadily. Most of the 90,000 Jews in Quebec are English-speaking, and over 200,000 Quebecers whose origins are in Europe, Africa, and Asia (including 100,000 whose ethnic roots are in France!) use English as their principal language. Some of these have immigrated twice, first to the Caribbean or the United States, and then to Quebec. An increasing proportion of English-speakers do not have white skin.[66]

Ethnic origin and place of birth are not the only elements of diversity in the English community. Even among Christians there is a division between Catholics and Protestants, and these two groups can be identified by their separate educational and health facilities as easily as by their churches. There are regional differences, too. Most English Quebecers live in or near Montreal, but important communities exist in other areas, in the Outaouais, the Eastern Townships, and the north shore of the St. Lawrence. There are English Quebecers in nearly every municipality in the province.

A very large number of English Quebecers have come from other provinces, the United States, and other parts of the world. They are not "native" English Quebecers, but individuals who were born and educated elsewhere and have decided that they would like to live in Quebec either permanently or for the time being. This is one of the most important factors in the differences of perception that exist between the English and the French, almost all of whom are "natives."

Some English Quebecers are rich, others are poor. The proportion at each income level is approximately the same as for the French-speaking community.[67]

Members of the English-speaking community, young and old, have made and continue to make an outstanding contribution to Quebec in every sphere. Until the second half of the twentieth century, the vast majority of job-creating projects in the industrial sector resulted from the initiatives of English Quebecers. Even today, the number of Quebecers employed by French-controlled and English-controlled manufacturing and mining activities is about equal.[68] To the well-known names of Molson, Bronfman, Price, and Webster must be added the thousands who have started and developed large, medium-sized, and small businesses of every kind, all of which have enriched Quebec.

The English contribution to Quebec goes much further than business. Important schools, universities, concert halls, hospitals, health care institutions, and churches and synagogues are the result of English initiatives. The list of distinguished English

Quebecers in every field of activity, past and present, is inexhaustible. Their contribution is visible today all over the province, particularly in Montreal. McGill University, the Montreal General Hospital, the *Gazette,* the Forum, the Queen Elizabeth Hotel, Place Ville Marie, Canadian Pacific, Alcan, Molson, the Museum of Fine Arts, and the Montreal Symphony Orchestra are only a few of the instantly recognizable names and places that are landmarks in the province. They were all developed, in large measure, by English Quebecers.

These English institutions benefit everyone. French-speaking people purchase insurance policies from Standard Life, just as English-speakers buy from La Laurentienne—and neither is diminished in the process.

The English of Quebec have a great tradition of service to the province and its people. Even English Quebecers motivated by self-interest have often indirectly created benefits for many others as well. There is no evidence that English businesspeople have ever been any less (or more) devoted to the interests of their employees, or their province, than are their French-speaking counterparts.

For some Quebecers it has become almost embarrassing to speak of this—as if anything that was not created in Quebec in French, by French-speaking Quebecers, should be forgotten—as if, in order to appear sincere, English Quebecers must pretend to be incompetent. But whether or not they prefer to talk about it, the English have made a very important contribution to Quebec life, and they continue to do so.

A Common Vision

The diversity of the English community is well known to its members. What has always been less clear are the elements that unify it. Much has been written on the subject[69] and some of it is contradictory, but a single element pervades. The members of the English community have one, and only one, common objective: they live, and wish to continue to live, in English. This is neither a political goal nor an article of some socio-cultural creed. It is the expression of an individual choice of language, made collective only by the need to create and maintain some common institutions.

Many English Quebecers would add that they also speak French or would like to, or that as English Quebecers they want to live closely with the French-speaking majority. But other members of the community do not share these priorities. The ability or desire to speak French is not part of the definition of an English Quebecer.

The English Quebecer is someone, regardless of country of birth, regardless of ethnic origin, who lives in English in Quebec and wishes to continue to do so. English Quebecers see language not as a cause, but as a personal choice, a natural right; and believe they should be allowed to exercise that right in Quebec.

English Quebecers cannot accept the premise that "Quebec is French," and only French, whether this is presented as a statement of truth or tactics. They cannot even accept the premise that they must necessarily "integrate" themselves into the society of the majority, however it is defined. There is plenty of space between isolation and integration, and somewhere in this space will be found the *terra firma* of relationships between the English and French communities in Quebec. We see two distinct societies in one political space.

Much has been said about the English community's obligation to the larger Quebec society. But, to the extent that these obligations exist, they fall equally heavily on all Quebecers, including the French. The English have no additional burden to bear.

They do have a responsibility for the future of their own community. The possibility of living in English exists only if a satisfactory institutional structure exists to support the language. There are some members of the French community who believe that the English should *not* exist as a recognized society in Quebec, and an even larger number who have not made up their minds on the question. But for those who choose to define themselves as English Quebecers and to remain as such, there is no choice. They must be committed to the maintenance of a distinct and officially recognized English community.

The most important challenge is to convince the English community to make this commitment, and in a new way. Since 1977 its leadership has been preoccupied with the process of negotiating a new social contract with the French community. Even though these efforts have so far had limited success, there is every reason why they should continue. But the new, main objective must be different. It must be designed to re-establish and build the confidence of the community in its ability to remain, grow, and contribute to Quebec society, in its. own language.

The best hope for a strong and confident English community is the presence of one that believes in itself and its own future and conveys this confidence to the rest of the world in a way that makes Quebec appealing to other English-speaking people.

The *second* objective of the English Quebecer is to seek accommodation with the French-speaking majority. The *first* is to remain strong, and grow, in English.

Where Are We Now?

There are some serious questions as to whether the will exists among the English community to reaffirm its presence. French Quebecers fear assimilation, but for the English community the corresponding danger is emigration. For anyone who speaks English, there are so many places to go, so many things to do. If the older members of the community are relatively immobile, their children and grandchildren are not. Many will leave Quebec simply to broaden their experience. Others will leave because they find better job opportunities, and good places to live, elsewhere.

There are fears about the future of English immigration as

well. Newcomers to Quebec are encouraged by the government to live in French, rather than in English. As a result, some of those who might come from English North America are deterred by what they perceive to be a hostile climate, in both senses of the expression. It is easy to be pessimistic about all this.

This prompts us to take a closer look at the current status of English Quebecers. Some claim that they are the most oppressed, others the most privileged, of all Canadians.

To some extent, the English are prevented from using their own language in Quebec today. The intentions expressed in the Charter of the French Language have been at least partly realized. But the authorities promised far more than they could ever hope to deliver. Many of the legislative powers required to impose a single language on the population do not lie within the competence of the provincial government. Federal laws apply in many sectors, including much of the communications, transportation, social security, and industrial sectors. The federal constitution guarantees a number of bilingual institutions and contains a charter of rights and freedoms that despite its loopholes puts important limits on the powers of both the federal and provincial governments.

Far more important, the largest part of the language activity of a citizen lies outside the control of any government in a democratic state. No laws can govern the language people use in the private intercourse that makes up most of their daily lives, at home, in the street, at work, and even in the schoolyards.

The English language is readily accessible in Quebec. In most areas there are plenty of English-speaking people to talk to, and most visitors to the province speak English. Magazines, books, films, radio, and television in English, made both in Quebec and in other parts of North America, are readily available. If proof of the accessibility of English is necessary, it is the fact that over 300,000 English-speaking residents of Quebec (46 percent of the total) tell the census takers that they speak no French at all.[70]

For those who wish to take advantage of it, there is the possibility of living fully in one of the few places in the world, certainly in one of the few cities, where two great language groups coexist in a generally fraternal and mutually supportive way. French Montreal is not Paris, and English Montreal is not New York or London, but quality of life is measured by more than the number of theatres, concert halls, and city parks. In its own way, Montreal provides a refreshing and civilized alternative that is unequalled by all but a few North American cities.

For all of these reasons, if English Quebecers were to analyse the restrictions on the use of their chosen language, they would discover that those restrictions are really quite limited and that Quebec holds enormous potential for anyone who wants a full and satisfying life. Hundreds of thousands of Quebecers like living here in English, and do so.

The English have been obliged to accept painful changes, as the French have occupied an important space in Quebec society that had, until recently, been of limited interest to them. Still, the picture that emerges of the situation today is one in which the English are essentially free to use their own language. The real constraint placed on this freedom is simply that they live in a place where eight out of ten of their neighbours are French-speaking.

One might imagine that every English person in Quebec is aware of being in the minority and would have reacted either by learning French, choosing a more limited life in the English community, or moving somewhere else. In fact, this is very nearly the situation that exists today.

Some English Quebecers who grew up in another time are still adjusting to the rapid changes they have lived through. Their minds have made the journey to a Quebec that is mainly French, but they find that their hearts are a bit more obstinate and difficult to control. But today nearly all English Quebecers realize that they share the province with a competent, powerful, and generally agreeable French-speaking community. They accept this as the cost, or the benefit (as the case may be), of living in Quebec. Their skill in the French language varies from person to person, and this influences the contacts they have with the members of the other group and the jobs to which they can aspire. But they accept this as a part of life here.

The Problem

What, then, is the problem? There are, in fact, two. First, the provincial government does have powers to control the use of a language in some activities that are very important in people's daily lives. And in a few of these activities the total "language space" is admittedly finite. In the process of sharing it, there must be winners and losers. For example, an increase in the use of French is often accompanied by a corresponding decrease in the use of English. The obligation to send children to French schools results in a reduced enrolment in English schools. Cinemas that are obliged to show French films do not show English films. Signs in French cannot be in English. In these cases, the government has been reducing the space available for English.

But this is not the heart of the problem. Some of these limitations have been accepted by the English community. The key question is, "Where does it end?" and no political party in Quebec has been prepared to face that question. There are some indications that the English are becoming institutionalized as scapegoats for a number of problems that the French-speaking society finds itself unable to solve.There are other indications that the real goal of the political elite, in both of the main political parties, is a gradual evolution to an entirely French-speaking society in Quebec.

There is simply no indication that in the long run the successive governments of Quebec, with the tacit approval of the French-speaking population, have had any linguistic goal other than the permanent expansion of the space occupied by the French language in Quebec. No limit, no stopping point, no acceptable state of equilibrium between the two groups has ever been formulated.

In other words the main problem has been, and remains, the uncertainty about the "status" of English Quebecers as articulated by the provincial government and French-speaking opinion leaders.

For many generations, up to the early 1960s, there was a *de facto* stability in the roles of the two linguistic communities in the social, political, cultural, and economic life of Quebec. With the coming of the Quiet Revolution, that situation changed radically. The French community began to abandon its traditional position in society and to interest itself in activities that had been dominated, until then, by the English.

This challenge by the French community received the enthusiastic support of the provincial government, which made the English community feel that the odds were being stacked against it. Its members still feel, more intensely than ever, that the Quebec government—their own government—is not on their side. Although this is presented as the affirmation of the French fact, it is understood by the English as an attack on them. And, directly or indirectly, that is what it is.

English Quebecers see themselves occupying a space that has been made considerably smaller by their own National Assembly in the last decade. They have, generally speaking, accepted this, but when they ask if there is any end to it, there is no reply from the government or from any political party. They see a lessening commitment by the Canadian federal parties to their community, and more and more, a weakening of the commitment of both English and French Canadians to maintain the federation as the pre-eminent political objective. Finally, it seems that not even the charters of rights and freedoms, both of Canada and of Quebec, can withstand the force of linguistic nationalism.

This is the central problem for English Quebec: a fully justified uncertainty about the future status of the community within the political framework of Canada and, above all, of Quebec. It is time to consider a solution to this problem.

The Goal

A journey can be more satisfying if one has some idea of either the final destination or the experiences and satisfactions to be sought along the way. So, before attempting to propose solutions to the problems of English Quebec, it might be helpful to describe the kind of situation in which the problems would cease to exist. What does English Quebec want?

English Quebec is first of all defined by the fact that it is and will remain a minority group. Therefore, for its members, an ideal situation would take into account the nature of their relationships with the French-speaking majority. But a more fundamental issue must be dealt with first. English Quebecers want the right to be English in Quebec and to have this right explicitly recognized by their government.

It should be possible for an English Quebecer who so desires, and who has the necessary ability, to live and work in English in Quebec, with the co-operation of the state. The perceived wisdom today would have it otherwise. Such isolation from the mainstream, such "lack of respect" for the majority, has come to be seen by the French-speaking elite, as well as by some members of the English community, as a condition to be condemned or ridiculed.

An English-speaking person, however, has no more responsibility to Quebec to speak French than a French-speaking person has a responsibility to Canada to speak English. These are private decisions. One can argue that to remain unilingually English in Quebec is wrong, short-sighted, and self-defeating. That is a valid point of view, but it is not the only one. The unilingual English Quebecer has the same personal rights and should command the same respect from the government as does the unilingual French Quebecer.

The notion that everyone in Quebec should, in principle, live and work in French was not always part of the accepted wisdom of the community. It is a way of seeing things that has evolved over the past two decades. But it is not an absolute truth. Nor is it a moral imperative or even, necessarily, a socially responsible thing to do. It is, in the final analysis, a fashion.

The level of bilingualism in Quebec is already one of the highest in the world. Still, 46 percent of the English and 70 percent of the French speak only one language.[71] The members of these groups who are unilingual, whether by choice or by circumstance, have the right to the respect of the state for their condition. And the state, within practical limits, should serve them in the language of their choice.

Unilingual English Quebecers are assured a limited and in some ways difficult life in a province whose population is massively French-speaking. They are unable to benefit from the most important advantage that living in Quebec offers. But the state should not be their enemy. A fundamental goal of the English community is to ensure that the government recognizes, and proclaims, the right to be English in Quebec.

This right of the individual to make a personal language choice applies not just to English, but to all languages. But beyond individual rights is the question of collective recognition. Here, the English community, because of its history and size, can justify its application for a distinct status. This claim has practical consequences in the modern state, which establishes and finances collective institutions of such fundamental importance as the educational and health care systems.

Many of Quebec's English institutions in these fields were established privately. Over time, they have been transferred to the public sector by legislation. They remain, for the most part, English in character; but their status, administration, and clientele are gradually being adjusted in a way that tends to make it progressively more difficult for the members of the English community to identify with them. The English wish to ensure that it remains possible for them to have their broken bones repaired, learn algebra, and take their leave of this world in their own language.

71

Another objective is a growing community. The English have always been a minority in Quebec. From a peak of 24 percent in 1861, they have gradually declined to 10 percent of Quebec's population in 1986. In absolute numbers, the English-speaking population has declined by 120,000 in fifteen years, a rate of 1 percentage point per year. Nothing can be more demoralizing to a community or more threatening to its institutions. And nothing will be more encouraging than a reversal of this trend. A perfectly legitimate goal of the English is to make their community grow. A reasonable objective now could be to recover the losses of the past fifteen years and to replace those 120,000 lost members of the community with new English Quebecers.

Most English Quebecers, with varying degrees of intensity, see themselves as Canadians too. In the independence debate of 1980 they were asked to choose between these two loyalties, and nearly all of them chose Canada. Since then, testing the relative strengths of their commitment to the two orders of government has become a major pastime for certain elements of Quebec society. The "real" Quebecer has been defined more and more narrowly, until there is hardly an English-speaker left who can identify with the model. The tests have not, it is true, been administered by the government itself. But editorialists,[72] opinion leaders, and politicians have expressed their conviction that loyalty to the "interests of Quebec" is the highest civic responsibility of every citizen living within its borders.

The persistence of these "purity tests" is more serious than the quality of the arguments themselves would imply. It not only suggests that there is one person or group that is competent to define these "interests" and "aspirations," it also implies that in a debate between Ottawa and Quebec, no loyal resident can ever argue that Quebec is wrong.

The intellectual underpinnings of this point of view are fragile; the moral basis is nonexistent. English Quebecers cannot accept it. They refuse the invitation to set aside their critical faculties when faced with an issue that divides the two governments of their federal system. Some of them may instinctively identify themselves with "Canada" more than with "Quebec." They are Quebecers just the same, and so are those for whom this choice is as irrelevant as choosing between one's right leg or left leg, and who believe that both are equally important to the work of standing erect in the world.

For English Quebecers, the province is a place where those who wish to feel strongly about Canada and its central government may be fully accepted, as can those who are more attached to Quebec and those who, for whatever reason, do not feel very strongly attached to either. In the final analysis, one should even have the right to remain silent in both languages.

There are, of course, collective goals as well. It is impossible to imagine an English community in Quebec living in isolation from the French majority. Most English Quebecers see their relationships with French Quebecers as a vital element in their own lives. Therefore, a high level of mutual acceptance, respect, and trust between the two groups, and a shared sense of belonging to a larger community, is another essential element in the definition of the English community in Quebec. It almost goes without saying that a prerequisite for achieving this condition is the ability of many members of the two communities to speak each other's language.

Finally, a shared sense of community implies shared projects. English and French Quebecers have many of these today. The members of both groups should work together, in a common "language," confidently, in business, in the community, and in government to build a more prosperous and just society in which there will be more space for the members of both groups. For the English in Quebec this is both a goal and a responsibility, and the only way to end the "winner–loser" mentality that pervades the language debate today.

The Environment

Equally important to the establishment of goals for a renewed English community is an understanding of the environment in which they must be realized.

Some members of the English community seem to suspect that somewhere there is a comprehensive plan, shared by all of the French-speaking elite, to gradually but firmly drive the English element in Quebec out of existence. At the other end of the spectrum are those, in daily contact with French-speaking colleagues and friends, who see this attitude as paranoia. They don't agree with the more extreme manifestations of French nationalism but see them as the public symptoms of a temporary state of insecurity, which will disappear as the emerging French society develops a higher degree of self-confidence and success. In the meantime they prefer not to disturb their satisfying relationships with individual French-speaking Quebecers by making the situation worse than it already is. In other words, there are important differences of perception within the English community about the environment in which it must face its future.

It is vitally important that we get this right. To succeed in making changes, we must understand the climate that surrounds us and have a true picture of the kinds of resistance and support we are likely to encounter. If we are blinded by resentment over perceived insults, obsessed by imaginary plots, or frozen in reaction, we could quite possibly make our situation worse. If, on the other hand, we choose to ignore the persistent weakening of the English community's position during the past two decades, we condemn ourselves to participate in its continuance.

What is the real situation? First, there is a powerful nationalist element in French Quebec. Within it is a much smaller group motivated by a personal vision of the past, which exercises real influence on the larger community. These individuals have come

74

to the conclusion that Quebec should be French only, and they do not care what happens to the English.

They use an outdated but still powerful vocabulary of "oppression" and "humiliation" and apply it indiscriminately both to their broad historical perspective and to incidents drawn from daily life. As they see it, the realization of their vision is impeded only by false ideas and sinister interests. These arguments are powerful, and they have a tendency to pass into the realm of *les choses qui se repetent* in the wider French-speaking community.

Most French Quebecers do not share this narrow and exclusive vision of their society. However, there is no element in the French-speaking majority that feels strongly that the English community needs, or deserves, support to remain a viable element in Quebec life. Some believe that English Quebecers should take care of themselves; all believe that they can.

The larger French-speaking community has a preoccupation with its own survival in North America. Its members instinctively react positively to every gesture or event that confirms or reinforces the French presence. If this results in the English community being diminished, it is not necessarily meant that way, but the result is not an important concern for the members of the majority group.

The members of the French-speaking community are deeply concerned with their own future. They accurately observe that if their own community exists today it is due not to the generosity of the English but to their own determination, over many generations, to keep it strong.

But there is no deliberate intention among the vast majority of French Quebecers to eliminate the English language or English community from their lives. They expect that the English, who they perceive as possessing considerable resources, will continue to assert themselves. They understand that the English community is weaker today than it was, but they expect it to resolve its own predicament.

Furthermore, many French Quebecers know that they must eventually make an accommodation with the other main language of North America in their own lives, in the lives of their children, and in the life of their community. The terms of this collective accommodation have not yet been established. The process of working it out has not even begun; but it will. At some point, the inadequacies of the Charter of the French Language—as the one and only instruction manual on language in Quebec—will become evident. At that moment, a new dialogue between English and French in Quebec will begin.

If this perception of the current environment is accurate, it means that the English community is not seen by most French Quebecers as something to be eliminated. Neither is it seen as a group in need of an aid program, or even as an asset for Quebec in an increasingly competitive world. For the time being, the English community must take care of itself, define itself, and assert itself. It must use all the resources it can develop to make itself strong. Then, from a position of confidence, it must be prepared to renew the negotiations on its role in Quebec when the moment arrives to do so.

4

COMING TO TERMS

. . . vous prononcez les mots aussi droit que les natifs d'Angleterre.

Je ne doute point d'apprendre, par la grace de Dieu, et un peu de temps.

Henry V
Act III, scene iv

The Vocabulary of the Environment

The social and political environment in Quebec, discussed in the last few pages of the previous chapter, is a complex thing. Before we propose a new approach for the English community, it should be examined a little more closely.

The English live as a minority in Quebec, in an environment that is not always easy for them to understand. It takes its shape in another language, and many of the emotions and even the words that form it do not translate very well.

The language of the language debate is part of the debate itself. A word such as "bilingualism," which is a simple noun in other parts of the world, is used as a weapon in Quebec. No one can be certain what Quebecers mean when they speak of "collective rights," "distinct society," and even "the English."

This is not the place to attempt a definitive dictionary of Quebec nationalism. However, a brief examination of some of these issues of "identity" will allow us a glimpse of the concerns and passions that lie within.

The choice is wide, but the subjects we will look at are:

— Is English a language or a community?

— Are the English the best-treated minority in Canada?

— Are collective rights more important than individual rights in Quebec?

— Is Quebec bilingual?

English: Language or Community?

A close look at the English question in Quebec shows that there are two related but quite distinct issues here. One issue concerns the English language, the other has to do with

78

the rights of minority communities. Each of these issues could exist without the other, and in some parts of the world they do.

First, there is the matter of the language itself. In many countries where the first language is not English, the authorities are preoccupied by its pervasive influence. In former British colonies such as India and Nigeria, it is seen rather positively, as a unifying force and as a means of communication with the modern world. In some of the developed countries, such as France, this ubiquitous language is seen as something of a threat. Whatever the perception, there is a preoccupation with English in a number of countries that have no indigenous English-language community at all.

The second issue, concerning the rights of linguistic minorities, is even more common around the world. We face it every day in our morning newpaper. For example, the Soviet Union, the countries of Eastern Europe, Finland, and almost all of Africa are homes for linguistic minorities. But in nearly all these cases, the minority language is not English but a more fragile tongue—Estonian, Serb, Swedish, Ibo. The external resources available to these linguistic minorities are generally quite limited. As a result, there tends to be popular sympathy for their cause in the international community and, quite often, at home.

In Quebec the two issues, "What to do about the English language" and "How do we treat our minorities," come together in a unique way, embodied in a single group of people.

On the question of the English language, the first reaction is to ask why it is a political issue at all. Surely the maintenance of linguistic security should be near the very bottom of any list of objectives for public policy in a free society. Why not let citizens get on with their affairs in the language of their choice? There is plenty of room for politicians to realize their ambitions within the traditionally accepted activities of government—the maintenance of law and order, the creation of public goods and services, and the redistribution of income.

It was the conception of the modern nation-state, two hundred years ago,[73] that changed all this and legitimized the intrusion of national governments into matters of language, religion, and ethnic origin, in the name of "the people." The rhetoric that evolved to justify it turned out to be highly useful in mobilizing the population for the pursuit of any number of common goals, both internal and external.

It also turned out to be highly dangerous. It has been observed that "the very word—nationalism—has the power of stopping thought."[74] Those who understand or have experienced the excesses of political nationalism have insisted that individual rights should predominate in national states and have tried to have them constitutionally defined in charters of rights and liberties. Quebecers, and all Canadians, have been extensively exposed to both sides of this debate in recent years.

French Quebecers are certainly not blind to the importance of human rights. It can, however, be argued that for over two centuries linguistic nationalism (allied until recently with religious nationalism) has defined the state of Quebec, more so than the land itself and more than the people who live here.

What are the consequences of such a political orientation? If the preservation of French is the ultimate political objective, then in a North American context, the other language, English, must become the ultimate political constraint.

Quebec governments and political parties have become expert in expounding the threat of the English language and mobilizing that threat for political objectives. The rhetoric that has been used and the legislative ramparts that have been erected are without parallel in the developed world. This threat is the justification for a language policy. Therefore the policy itself is, essentially, not a program to extend the use of French, but to try somehow to limit the use of one, and only one, language, English. The force of English is a preoccupation in other parts of the world; in Quebec it is an obsession.

On the surface, this is a surprising state of affairs. If there is one place in the world that clearly needs English it is Quebec, situated as it is in North America. Most of its people live within a few minutes' drive of the United States or Ontario, where English is almost the only language of communication. A Quebec open to the rest of the world is essentially a Quebec open to the English language. Throughout North America, French is of limited use to Quebecers once they leave their province. English happens to be, for the moment at least, the pre-eminent modern language, the lingua franca of technology and research, and the language of an America that reinvents it every day in a most dynamic way and uses it to transmit the world's most popular culture.

Most French-speaking Quebecers are fully aware of this, but they have decided to remain French-speaking. They do not propose to keep their language alive only in the home, or as something to enrich their cultural life. They would like to make it, in the words of the Charter of the French Language, "the normal and everyday language of work, instruction, communication, commerce, and business."

However, the "normal and everyday language" of much of the developed world is English. And, unlike the situation that prevails in most other non-English countries, the intensity with which it is used is at its highest on the very borders of Quebec.

This is another unique element in Quebec's situation. Sweden, for instance, has as many people as Quebec, and English is not its language either. But on Sweden's borders the people speak Norwegian or Finnish or Danish, and beyond the frontiers of those countries the language is German and Russian. In Sweden the English "menace" arrives by airplane, a few hundred businesspeople or tourists at a time, not along a vast border. In North America, even if there is no plan on the part of the English to impinge on the French language in Quebec, it happens anyway, across a linguistically undefendable frontier.

The response to this situation, by all political parties and by the leaders of all sectors of the French-speaking community, is to portray the future of the French language in Quebec as bleak, even desperate. Using a vocabulary perfected over two hundred years, each group seeks new ways to expose the threat of English from "outside," whether from assimilation, the power of American television, or the threat of new immigrants. The picture of a small and threatened minority in an enormous and unconsidering universe of English has been engraved on each new generation of French-speaking Quebecers.

The province's French-speaking leadership has concluded that in order to succeed in keeping Quebec French, there must inevitably be an organized and intensive struggle against the sea of English in which they swim, a struggle that can never end.

This fascination with the English language on the part of French Quebecers is not reciprocated. Those in North America who speak English do not feel threatened by the French language; neither do they have the disappearance of French in Quebec as one of their goals. It is not even an issue.

In the past there may have been some English-speaking Quebecers who hoped that French would disappear. But it is impossible to find even one person in Quebec today who has this goal. These thoughts, if they exist at all, belong to the realms beyond fantasy, as do the fears of those who believe that such a plot might exist. No one in North America has a plan, or even the wish, to get rid of French in Quebec.

Clearly, the arguments for language legislation in Quebec are not based on the belief that such a plan exists. But it is important to make this point to illustrate that the struggle is not really between two opposing groups of people, but between a group on one side and a phenomenon, a way of life, on the other. It is extremely difficult, however, for politicians to wage battles with a "phenomenon." It must be personalized, and this imperative leads us inescapably to the second issue, that of the English community in Quebec.

If the English language outside Quebec represents a massive threat to the French community, then surely the presence of "the English" inside—with their newspapers, television and radio stations, businesses, schools and institutions, and their insistence on speaking English—is an additional concern. It is the present, internal, and personalized manifestation of the larger external problem.

Most French-speaking Quebecers seem to believe that the English community has a right to be in Quebec. But nearly all of them believe that it should be controlled and restricted and that its behaviour should be "respectful" and consistent with its minority status. There are also those who believe that the time has come to show the English who is now "the boss."

There are constraints on these ambitions. The Canadian federation was established on the principle that there are two recognized language groups, and one of these is English. Certain collective rights are guaranteed in the constitution,[75] and others are so well established as to make their removal practically impossible. The traditions of democratic societies are values shared by French-speaking Quebecers, and they are enshrined in both the Quebec and the Canadian charters of rights and freedoms.

Furthermore, Quebecers are extremely sensitive to what is written about them abroad. The behaviour of the French-speaking community toward its largest minority group does not pass unnoticed in the international community, particularly the very important part of it that considers the English language to be a thing of unquestionable beauty. To those people, the restriction of English in Quebec is akin to the restriction of geometry.

But, constraints notwithstanding, the only element of this worldwide English phenomenon over which the Quebec authorities have some jurisdiction, the only bit of it on which they can illustrate the struggle and their determination to win, is the English-language community within Quebec's borders. As a result, this group has become the symbol of a larger problem. And each small victory over the English in Quebec, even though it is usually a victory over the wrong enemy, gives encouragement to the French community that it can prevail in what is seen as an almost universally hostile linguistic environment.

The French community uses, and intends to continue to use, as its principal tongue a language that will be of rather limited use to it outside its own borders and the national capital region. The alternative language is English, which is seen as awesomely seductive. So there is a determination to keep Quebec French, not bilingual, in the belief that the language must remain massively relevant at home, at least.

This pertinence must be illustrated by symbolic, as well as practical, gestures. In fact, the symbolic ones are in some ways preferred because they require less time and effort and are rich in rhetorical dividends. Furthermore, victories over the English are the easiest to win, because that community is the one part of the English-language phenomenon that cannot say "no" to the government of Quebec.

It is as if, when faced with a bitterly cold night outside one's door and helpless to do anything about it, one tries to obtain some small revenge by disconnecting the refrigerator.

Canada's French Minorities

One of the obstacles to understanding the political issues facing the English in Quebec is the tendency of both sides in the debate to make comparisons with the French minorities in the rest of Canada. The notion that the English in Quebec and French minorities in the other provinces are analogous and have the same problems, to which the same solutions must be applied, has inspired an avalanche of rhetoric by both sides in the debate ever since it was introduced in the federal government's Official Languages Act in 1969.

Are the English in Quebec the best- or the worst-treated minority in Canada? It depends on how one looks at it. Seen from the perspective of the space occupied by their language and institutions, they are certainly the most fortunate. Seen from the perspective of their status within provincial law, they are probably in second place, after bilingual New Brunswick.

From the perspective of what the provincial government does to encourage them, they are certainly the least favoured. In other provinces, current government policy is (with varying degrees of enthusiasm) to help the French minorities. In Quebec, the official policy of the provincial government is to reduce the role of the English.

The point is (and on this the most ardent English and French nationalists could agree) that the issues facing the English minority in Quebec and the French minorities in the rest of Canada are two different issues. They are both important, they both go to the heart of the definition of Canada, but they are as different from each other as the issue of the Native peoples is from both of them.

In other regions of Canada the minority language is French, and it is safe to say that no one needs that language to live a full and successful life in his or her own town or province. French-speaking families in Alberta and even, for the most part, New Brunswick do not see French as their only language but as one of two, and most understand its value for them to be essentially cultural, in the wider sense of the term.

Furthermore, with a few notable exceptions, the French minority communities in the other provinces of Canada did not create an array of powerful private educational and health institutions and bring them into the public network. Most of their French-language institutions have been recently created by the public sector in response to a growing sense of responsibility for these communities.

Finally, there is virtually no assimilation on the part of English Canadians *into* the French communities of Nova Scotia or Saskatchewan. Quite the opposite.

Consider, however, the English in Quebec. They are a minority, but their language is the most popular on earth, for reasons that have little to do with Quebec itself. It is nearly impossible to communicate with anyone in the United States and Canada, outside of Quebec, in a language other than English. Many French Quebecers who do not speak English have children who will. The English in Quebec developed a full educational infrastructure on their own initiative long before the Quebec government created a department of education. The same applies in the health sector and in many other fields.

How did two such different problems get themselves attached to a single solution? The history of the linguistic battle for Canada has been traced in a number of texts, and the bitter memory of it lingers on for French Quebecers. To put it in its simplest form, Quebec was won for the French and the rest of Canada was won for the English. At least that is the current situation, and almost everyone would agree that, if the battle is not over, then the odds on a possible territorial expansion by the French are very long indeed.

It was within this context that the bilingual policies of the early Trudeau governments were developed. The objective was to redress the weakness of the French-speaking minority in Canada and to restore the principle of linguistic duality on which the country was founded, with the central government as its guardian. For a number of reasons of symmetry and politics, the English minority in Quebec became an element of this policy. But the symmetry of the policy relating to the two groups was not supported by a corresponding symmetry in the situation.

The English in Quebec are the most fortunate linguistic minority in Canada, not by virtue of any policies of their provincial government, but because of their own past efforts and because of the ocean of English in which they swim. At the same time, the Quebec government has the most restrictive policies regarding its linguistic minorities of any government in Canada, not because it is inherently mean or ethnocentric, but because English in Quebec has not in the past required encouragement by the public sector in the same way that French does in Ontario.

In other words, the English of Quebec are the most fortunate and the least favoured of minorities.

When the premier of Quebec states that the English in Quebec are the most privileged minority in Canada he should add that it is, for him, an historical error, and that his government is doing what it can to "correct" the situation. And when the

English complain that the national policies for encouraging bilingualism do not seem to apply to them, they would be wise to recall that these policies were never established with them in mind in the first place, no matter what federal politicians may say from time to time.

The English in Quebec will not be saved by Canada's official-language policies or by the expansion of French services in British Columbia. Their problem is partly a Canadian problem, but its provincial dimension must be approached by the Quebec government and by Ottawa in a unique way.

The provincial government shows that it understands this when it consistently refuses to support the claims of the French minorities in the other provinces for the expansion of their constitutional rights.[76] It fears that this would strengthen the position of its own English minority.

A linguistic policy for Quebec must be made in Quebec. It must be based on Quebec's own vision of a civil society, on a program to protect the French language, on a recognition in practical terms of the rights of the English community, on a realistic appraisal of the importance of English in external communications for all Quebecers, and on the impact that Quebec's language policy has on its reputation in the international community.

From the federal government, the English community requires a separate, active program of help, but not one based on a notion of the symmetry of the official languages. It is required because the English live in a province whose government is consistently attempting to enlarge its own powers at the expense of the central government, and at the same time make the province more French, at the expense of its most important minority. The federal government can counterbalance these efforts in two ways: by continuing to insist on full bilingualism within Quebec in its own fields of constitutional jurisdiction, and by making sure that, in consultation with English Quebecers, it puts in place a program for them that goes to the heart of their unique situation.

Individual and Collective Rights

When facing language issues, the English and the French do not see "human rights" in the same way. The experience of Bill 178 casts a spotlight on these divergent visions, and recalling this event provides useful information in the development of a strategy for the English community.

Charters of human rights and freedoms are designed to protect the individual against abuses of power by other individuals and institutions. But they are most pertinent, and are designed to be so, in the not infrequent cases of the individual versus the state.

A number of countries have adopted charters of human rights, many of them inspired by the United Nations' Universal Declaration of Human Rights.[77] Two elements often found within them are clauses that guarantee "freedom of expression" and "freedom from discrimination" on the basis of language, religion, or ethnic origin.

In 1975 Quebec's Liberal government adopted a charter of rights that was acknowledged to be a very enlightened one, and it included these two elements in its charter. So the province did not object, in principle at least, when the federal government included similar clauses in its Charter of Rights and Freedoms in the constitutional amendments of 1981.

However, facing, and often opposing, the charters of rights there is language legislation, now considered to be as permanent a feature of the Quebec landscape as the St. Lawrence River. Almost by definition, language laws are likely to involve some limitation on freedom of expression.

When the Parti Québécois adopted its language legislation in 1977, its original intention was that this legislation would override the Quebec Charter of Human Rights and Freedoms. However, under intense pressure from the Liberal opposition it changed the proposed bill and made it subordinate to the charter.

The acting leader of the Liberal opposition, Gérard D. Levesque, said at the time, "I can only say that we are fully in agreement with the change. . . . The Liberal deputies believe it is essential to reconcile the provisions of the language legislation with those of the Charter of Human Rights and Freedoms."[78]

Eleven years later, in 1988, the Liberal government found itself face to face with the consequences of Levesque's statement of principle. To the casual observer, a law that forbids the English, or the Italians, or anyone except the French, to put up a sign in their own language is probably a limitation on freedom of expression, and it is certainly a case of discrimination based on language. The courts thought so too, unanimously, as the question was raised successively in the Superior Court of Quebec, the Quebec Court of Appeal, and the Supreme Court of Canada. But the signs law was adopted, "notwithstanding."

How could this happen? How could an entire population, after equipping itself with a written charter that clearly established one standard of justice for all its citizens, approve an act that clearly and unambiguously violated that standard? How could Gérard D. Levesque, who knew exactly what was at stake, stand his own logic on its head?

We have already mentioned some of the rationalizations that were used for this move. The English in Quebec, Canada, and around the world were shocked, and Messrs. French, Marx, and Lincoln resigned over the issue. But what lessons can be drawn for the future?

The most important one is that, until further notice, the parts of both the Canadian and Quebec charters that protect citizens against discrimination on the basis of the language they use are likely to be inoperative in Quebec, in the face of a much more powerful impulse to expand the use of French. Another lesson is that the provincial government, supported by the French-speaking population, will fight to maintain laws that permit it to expand French, notwithstanding the individual's right to freedom from discrimination.

This is the way things are. It does not mean that the

charters are worthless or that the French-speaking citizen is not as sensitive as anyone else to other abuses of human rights. But, when the French language is in question, there is a loyalty to "community" in the French population of Quebec that is likely to be stronger than the loyalty to the concept of human rights.

A justifiable collective right is generally understood to be the extension of an individual right to an institution that is considered necessary to the realization of that right. An English-speaking person—*any* person—would acknowledge the validity of this concept. The right to be educated in English must logically be extended to include the right to have an English school system. The right to free choice of religion implies the right to construct a church, temple, or mosque and to worship together.

But a commercial sign, or even a street full of them, cannot be considered an "institution" without stretching the meaning of the word beyond recognition. The denial of someone's right to erect a sign that says "Flowers" cannot be justified as the collective extension of someone else's right to put up a sign saying "Fleurs." This vision of collective rights goes beyond any judicial interpretation and can be defended only by recourse to what seems, to most English Quebecers, to be a highly simplistic vocabulary of political nationalism, or of opportunism.

For French Quebec, on the other hand, it seems quite normal. A typical illustration of that point of view is the following extract from a column in *La Presse*. Writing at the time of the adoption of the signs law, Francine Pelletier argued that "by insisting on their democratic rights and on freedom of expression" the English leadership had "insulted" the French Quebecer. She added that

> Above all, their words had shown that, right or wrong, in the final analysis, the English always end up choosing Canada, its privileges and its enviable sense of democracy. But francophones, even the most federalist among us, always end up choosing Quebec, its eventful history, and

90

its skin-deep insecurity. This is exactly where one sees the difference between francophones and anglophones.[79]

It should be noted that Pelletier was writing, not about anything that English Quebec had done, but about a decision of the Supreme Court of Canada that was based on Quebec's own Charter of Human Rights and Freedoms.

It is doubtful that the members of Quebec's English community can be mobilized to adopt, fully and enthusiastically, the "francophone" vision as their own. But to live successfully in Quebec, they should learn to accept it as a fact of life and, to some extent, make use of it for their own purposes.

English Quebecers should be aware that the struggle for their own language will not be won, or even played, on the field of individual human rights. To be understood in Quebec politics, English-speaking Quebecers and the leaders of their institutions must learn and use the vocabulary of collective action and collective rights in a way that their cousins in the rest of North America would find unnecessary and even incomprehensible.·

The English are unaccustomed to the collective struggle required to ensure the existence of a minority community. Their identity as Quebecers is diluted by emotional and practical ties with Canada or North America. Their instinctive affiliation with the rights of the individual makes them unlikely soldiers in the army of a "language community."

But although conscription is out of the question, the numbers of those who share this sense of common purpose in the English community must grow. Otherwise, faced with the collective energy of the French-speaking majority in Quebec, they have only two other alternatives: to leave, or to remain as part of what will slowly but surely become an "expatriate" community, divested of its own institutions in an encounter lost for lack of players.

Bilingualism

There are probably few places on earth where a higher proportion of the population speaks two languages than in Quebec. In the most recent census, more than 30 percent of French Quebecers said they spoke English, and almost 60 percent of English Quebecers affirmed that they were able to express themselves in French.[80]

Everywhere in Quebec, one sees evidence of two languages. Radio and television bring them into every living room in the province. French and English newspapers, magazines, and films are easily available. In Montreal, the economic and cultural centre of the province, the two languages are so mixed in daily use that many people are hardly aware of which one they are using at any given moment. In other words, Quebec is bilingual.

The French-speaking leaders of Quebec, those in politics, the arts, and the economy, recognize the importance of knowing two languages. Almost all of them are bilingual, and many of them make sure their children are bilingual too, because they know that facility in these two languages brings not only a heightened cultural sensibility, but power as well. Bilingual people earn more, and more opportunities are open to them.

So it would seem that all is well. In a society that requires two languages, the people are bilingual. On the premise that most reasonable people believe the knowledge of two important languages to be better than knowing only one, it might be imagined that the authorities in Quebec would promote bilingualism as a positive feature of that society, as many Quebecers do for their own children. Every resident would be encouraged to learn both languages. Immigrants—who by virtue of their decision to leave home are likely to be disposed to learn new tongues—would be encouraged to come to a place where they could learn two of them. Investors from both English- and French-speaking countries could be welcomed and made to feel at home, understanding that French was the principal language of the workplace and that English could be used as well.

It is astounding to observe that none of this is happening. The political and intellectual elite are not only against a bilingual Quebec, they consistently claim, despite all evidence to the contrary, that it does not even exist. They insist that "Quebec is French," as if the statement repeated often enough will change the very nature, not only of Quebec, but of its continental environment.

Thus a real advantage of Quebec society is turned into a major limitation. Because the English language is presumed to have a much greater attraction, bilingualism is considered to be an unstable and impermanent condition, a brief stopping point on the road to linguistic assimilation. It is as if the leaders of the French-speaking community believe that English is a virus that kills French on contact, or that the French Canadian is incapable of functioning in two languages.

A recent minister of education, Claude Ryan, who speaks excellent English himself, has expressed serious reservations about teaching this second language to French children. He says, "English is the language of North America and . . . we've long understood that premature exposure to English might not be compatible with the best development of the child."[81]

This approach has astonishing consequences. For instance, the average earnings of a bilingual worker in Quebec are higher than those of someone who speaks only French or English.[82] Incredibly some claim that this proves discrimination against the unilingual French person and that the government has a responsibility to correct the situation. It is difficult to imagine another place in the developed world where such an attitude to the knowledge of two languages could exist.

In an attempt to remove bilingualism from the political vocabulary of Quebec, a number of efforts have been made to persuade the population that "Quebec is French." In 1974 the

Liberal government of Robert Bourassa used legislation to make French the only official language of Quebec. Whether or not this was a good idea, it was certainly something the government had the right to do.

What was not made clear, however, was that French thereby became the official language, not of Quebec, but only of the provincial government and its administrative bodies. Even this policy was limited by provisions in the Canadian constitution that declare French *and English* to be the official languages of the provincial legislature and courts. French certainly did not become the official language of those activities in Quebec that fall within the jurisdiction of the federal government, where bilingualism is the rule.

In 1977 the Charter of the French Language went further and declared its intention to make French the "normal and everyday language of work, instruction, communication, commerce and business." But even this law was unable to achieve such a goal, because much of the activity in question lay outside the competence of the provincial, or of any, government.

Despite all its laws and declarations, Quebec has been and remains a bilingual province. It is difficult to conclude that its residents are any the worse for it. However, the only group in Quebec currently encouraged by the government to be bilingual is the English community.

Might we dream that the day will come when "bilingual" and "bilingualism" become positive words in the political vocabulary of Quebec, when the rhetoric will reflect the reality? Then, the leaders of the French majority will accept their responsibility to provide the same linguistic opportunities to the French-speaking population, and new Quebecers, that they now give to English Quebecers—the opportunity and the encouragement to understand both French and English.

When this happens, English-speaking Quebecers will find new allies. In the meantime, the current government attitude—that only the English should be encouraged to use both languages and that everyone else should speak only French—will continue to provide the English with the opportunity to exercise an influence in Quebec that is considerably greater than their numbers would imply.

AFFIRMATION

All things are ready, if our minds be so.

Henry V
Act IV, scene iii

We're On Our Own

This chapter proposes a new approach to living in English in Quebec. The preceding pages should have made clear the need for it. Quebec's English community is faced with a continuing decline in numbers and in strength. We have failed in our efforts to convince the French-speaking majority and the provincial government that they should help us to arrest this decline, to define the English community's place in Quebec society, and to encourage its healthy growth in the province.

The proposed new approach has been made necessary by circumstances determined mainly by the French-speaking majority. Paradoxically, it draws its inspiration from the same source. If French Quebecers have managed to retain and develop a vibrant minority community in North America it has not been through the goodwill of others, but by relying on their own resources, cohesion, and determination. They do not exist as a viable community in Quebec today because the English wanted it that way; they have done it, over three hundred years, *themselves.*

Some might claim that during this period the English have displayed tolerance and collaborated with their French-speaking neighbours. No one, however, can make the case that the English ever worked to build a strong French-speaking community in Quebec.

We would be extremely naive to think that the growth of the English community can be achieved in any other way. Eventually we will have to reach an understanding with the French community that will be beneficial for both groups. But it can do this only if our own community is confident, self-reliant, cohesive, determined, and strong.

The French-language community does have an image of us that it would like us to adopt as our own. But if we accept it, we are doomed to unending attenuation. We should not actively participate in the disintegration of our own community. We must, calmly and with disrespect for no one, do our own thing.

The language debate in Quebec is essentially *a peaceful struggle for space and power*—economic, political, social, and cultural. In some respects the total space available to both communities is limited, which means that sometimes there will be winners and losers. This is the most divisive part of the struggle—over places in schools, who gets a specific job, the wording on signs.

In other ways, however, the space is infinitely expandable, and there can be winners without losers. Learning one language does not mean that the other one cannot be used. If the two communities work together to create a more prosperous and growing community, there is more space—more jobs and more cultural activity—for both groups. This is the creative part of the struggle.

But in either case it is a struggle for space and power. Those who do not like this word may prefer to call it "healthy competition," but surely no one can deny its existence. And a realistic appraisal of population statistics and the life around us leads to the conclusion that for the past two decades the English have been losing this struggle, slowly but surely, and they are still losing today.

The English community can remain and grow in Quebec, but English-speaking Quebecers must make it happen. The power of the English language *outside* Quebec will not be sufficient to ensure the growth of the English community *in* Quebec. English Quebecers must undertake the personal and collective action necessary to ensure their own revival. They must put aside the tedious vocabulary of "integration," "isolation," "oppression," "repression," "respect," "contempt," "majority," and "minority." They must take the initiative and build a stronger and larger community for themselves, with their own resources, "as if they did not have a friend in the world."[83] They must proceed calmly and confidently, believing in themselves and their own future in Quebec.

Many English Quebecers say they are tired of debating the language question. There is no need to continue it; the debate has already taken place. It is now necessary to act. This will be a new experience for many, but the alternative, in the face of the cohesiveness and determination of the French-speaking majority, is the continued erosion of Quebec's English population and its institutions.

The unique experience of living in English in Quebec is not cost-free. It requires a heightened sense of collective responsibility from a group whose instincts, developed over generations of successful individual effort, are averse to collective initiatives. English Quebecers may individually find it relatively easy to live their lives in English; but unless they also have a sense of collective responsibility it is highly unlikely that their children will be here to enjoy the same advantages.

This means that the English community, especially its leaders, will have to maintain a strong sense of dedication, not only to institutions, schools, and hospitals, *but to the language itself.*

Fortunately, there are many who already do. The community has developed a much stronger sense of its unique position in Quebec during the past fifteen years. But the urge to move a few miles away to a place where the struggle is unnecessary, or to stay but refuse to engage the French majority in a way that respects their collectivist terms of reference, are attractive alternatives for those who feel that the language debate is a constricting, even suffocating, exercise. The younger English Quebecer, already bilingual and integrated into the larger life of the province, can be particularly difficult to convince.

But the future of the community depends on this effort. So far, the French-speaking majority has set no limit to the expansion of French in Quebec. What it seeks, explicitly in some cases and implicitly in others, is simply a French Quebec. The only part of it that will remain English is the part that the English occupy and refuse to vacate.

Mutual accommodation is possible. Although there are a number of countries where destructive language conflicts persist, there are also places—Finland, Switzerland, and the evolving

European Community come to mind—where different language groups live together in harmony, their differences largely resolved and their positions mutually acknowledged by a combination of laws, institutions, time, and good will.

No foreign solution can be applied directly to the Quebec situation, but these experiences at least show that language differences can be turned into a positive force. However, this can only occur if each group is determined and organized, understands the limits of its power, and knows how to use what it has, peacefully, both in its own interests and for the whole community.

The Equality Party and the 1989 Election

There are already some important indications that the English community has arrived at a new level of understanding itself. The most interesting of these recently has been the creation, and initial success, of the first political party that represents only the English.

In the weeks that followed the adoption of the signs law and the resignation of French, Marx, Lincoln, and Orr, the community was faced with a leadership vacuum. There were serious questions as to how, or whether, it would be filled.

The answer to those questions was not long delayed. Stimulated by the knowledge that there was to be a general election in Quebec in the near future and faced with the certainty that the Liberal Party would not modify its position on language, two new "English" political parties appeared: the Equality Party, essentially a Montreal group; and the Unity Party, whose roots were in rural Quebec. Their approach was simple and clear. With no time to propose a complete political program, they offered English Quebecers an opportunity to protest in a very tangible way against a political decision that had angered them. In providing this opportunity, they made it possible to evaluate clearly the extent of that anger.

It was clear that the overwhelming majority of the English community was opposed to the signs legislation, but it was less certain that this opposition could be translated into votes in an election. Some English voters had larger loyalties to the Liberal Party. Others would not support a single-issue party. There were some who feared that splitting the federalist vote would aid the Parti Québécois and its goal of independence. There were also a number of Liberal candidates who enjoyed a high level of personal popularity. Finally, the organizations of the new parties were rudimentary, and it was difficult to obtain candidates with established reputations.

However, the leaders of the two parties learned their new trade rapidly, and their prospects were boosted by Alliance Quebec when its chairman, Peter Blaikie, urged the English community to vote for anyone *but* the Liberals or the Parti Québécois.

On election day, November 18, 1989, the Equality and Unity parties presented candidates in 35 of the 125 ridings in Quebec (18 in Montreal). When the voting was over, two-thirds of the English community in counties with English-party candidates had voted for them[84] and the Equality Party had won the four Montreal ridings with the largest English populations. In the Westmount and Jacques Cartier ridings the Liberals had previously held the seats for over fifty years. In D'Arcy-McGee (where the Equality Party leader was elected) and Notre-Dame-de-Grâce, no one but a Liberal had won an election there since the ridings had been created. In another seven counties, the English parties won over 20 percent of the vote. In a total of 19 Quebec ridings, more than 10 percent of all voters supported the English parties.[85]

After the election the leader of the Equality Party, Robert Libman, announced the fusion of the Equality and Unity parties into one organization and began the difficult process of leading his group of four members of Quebec's first English-language political party in the National Assembly.

The most important news that emerged from the election

results was that the desire to protest against the Liberal government was not limited to the more extreme elements of the English community (the "freedom of choice" advocates), as had been the case in 1976. This time there was broad support, sufficient to win some seats.

This was an important change. Some members of the English community suffered more than others from the events of the past twenty years. The young and well-educated found it relatively easy to adapt to a new, bilingual, integrated way of life. They were even, at times, critical of those members of their own community who did not want to change or did not know how to. Just as the more nationalist members of the French community were developing their model of a "real" Quebecer, some members of the English elite were busy defining the "real" English Quebecer—bilingual, integrated, open to the "new reality" of Quebec.

The elections showed that this division within the English community did not run very deep. The decision to vote for a protest party, Equality or Unity, came more naturally to unilingual English Quebecers, while many "integrated" members of the community found the decision difficult. But nearly all the English could understand the cause and, despite past loyalties and the evident limitations of the new political parties, two-thirds of the community voted for a new party on election day.

The English community, faced with a serious crisis, had demonstrated that it could respond, effectively, in a united way. In the 1970s the English succeeded in developing their own community organizations. At the end of the 1980s they created their own party and belatedly entered the world of tribal politics, an inescapable feature of collective life in Quebec.

Where Do We Go From Here?

In trying to determine the next steps for English Quebec it is useful to examine the equipment that each side brings to this peaceful struggle for space and power.

The French community has two important advantages. The first is, obviously, size. When 83 percent of the population is French, when many regions of Quebec are almost entirely so, when private and public institutions of all kinds, including the National Assembly, are overwhelmingly French, then any minority community is faced with a problem in simply maintaining the minimum numbers necessary for its own survival.

The second advantage of the French-speaking community is the support it receives from the provincial government, which is publicly committed to maintaining and expanding the influence of the French majority. The many steps the government has taken in support of the project need not be repeated here. However, it is worth noting that, so far as language legislation is concerned, the government has probably now exhausted the practical options open to it.

The public sector cannot become more French-speaking than it already is. In the parapublic sector, it is conceivable that limitations could be applied on admission to English colleges and universities. But this is probably impractical, considering the traditions on which the system is based and the mobility of high school graduates.

Furthermore, the government has probably gone about as far as it can by way of intervention in the private sector. Consideration has been given to extending the compulsory francization programs to small companies, but this is fraught with administrative problems and short-term costs in competitiveness. Signs cannot be more French than they are now.

The telecommunications and broadcasting fields fall under federal jurisdiction, to the extent that they can be controlled at all, given Quebec's proximity to the United States. The right to distribute English-language publications could scarcely be challenged, and there is no way for the government to control the language of private conversation.

It appears likely, then, that apart from the renaming of streets and villages, the legislature's language machine is out of gas, at least so long as Quebec is a part of Canada. The administration of some existing laws could, perhaps, be tightened up; but there is little space for new ones.

Those laws already in place are an important constraint on the English. But, rhetoric apart, we need not expect much more coercive language activity from the government of Quebec in the years immediately ahead. It has done what it could, and we are still here.

However, in the short term it is unlikely that the government will relax existing rules or that the English will be able to obtain more space and power from the provincial legislature. The goal must be to find it elsewhere, to create new power from other sources.

Speaking English

What equipment does the English community bring to the struggle? It is not without resources. By far the most import-ant—and this would be acknowledged by both sides—is the strength and the attractiveness of the English language and the fact that it is one of the two official languages of the Canadian federation.

The English language and the right to use it are the most important assets we have in any effort to make our community grow. Used wisely, they are extremely powerful tools. It is by extending the use of English that we will build the community.

English Quebecers should use English, wherever and when-ever they can, without any hesitation or feeling of guilt. In doing so, they will reinforce the language and support the efforts of their fellow English-speaking citizens, who are doing the same thing. The French community has taught them that the more a language is used, the stronger it will become.

In doing so, English Quebecers will discover that English can be used, and used widely. Despite all they may have heard, and despite the fact that 83 percent of the population speaks French, Quebec itself is not French, not even officially. The only thing that is officially French is the Quebec government, and it has already been pointed out that this situation is a qualified one.

Most importantly, the decision to speak or write in any language is essentially a private decision. Governments cannot legislate what they cannot control, and no one can supervise the private language practices of six and a half million Quebecers. With the marginal exception of commercial signs, no government has even tried to make Quebecers use French in their private lives.

Furthermore, there is no moral or ethical reason why people should not speak and live in English in Quebec. It was never preordained that the land north of the Ottawa and St. Lawrence rivers should be entirely French-speaking. The land has been "promised" to no one, and if most of Quebec is French-speaking today it is simply because that community has been more energetic and effective in maintaining its presence than have the English.

English Quebecers should insist, politely but firmly, on their right as consumers, in the stores and on the telephone, to be served in their own language, and to use their own language at work. We should not feel the least bit guilty about speaking English. We should use and enjoy the language and encourage others to speak it as well.

The Charter of the French Language says that "consumers of goods and services have a right to be informed and served in French." That statement of what should be obvious was written into law because, for decades, French-speaking consumers did not insist on their right to be served in their own language. English Quebecers should not make the same mistake.

The right to be served in one's own language exists for the English, too, if they wish to exercise it. Stores and businesses whose clientele insist on being served in English will continue to provide that service. There is nothing in any language legislation that forbids people to ask for, receive, and give service in English or any other language, and Quebec does not require a law to ensure the use of English on the streets of our province. It will be there if people insist, politely but firmly, on using it.

Youth and Jobs

In the language debate, the most important issue for most people, and especially for young English Quebecers, is the language of work. Here, too, let it be understood that there is plenty of space for English today, and even more to be claimed.

An examination of Quebec's language legislation reveals a "fundamental language right," of uncertain juridical force, that states that "workers have a right to carry on their activities in French."[86] There is also a chapter relating to the language of labour relations, on which has been built a regulatory program to increase the use of French in firms with over fifty employees. The law also establishes the right of customers to be served in their own language and the obligation of management to communicate in writing in French with the government and with workers who desire it. For those who wish to work in English there are, of course, practical constraints as well. Most of the Quebec market is French-speaking and so are most workers.

All of this would seem to pose a formidable barrier to working in English. But there are a number of other factors to consider. First, the vast majority of Quebec firms employ fewer than fifty people and therefore are not subject to francization programs. Much more important, even employees of companies that are subject to these programs still manage to speak a great deal of English.

Nearly all Quebec firms do business—buy, sell, and get new ideas—outside the province. To do this, English is essential. Quebec's economy will always be an open one. As a result, there is a great deal of English spoken in business in Quebec, and the provincial government is fully aware that this must continue. The absence of more extensive language control in the workplace also reflects the practical impossibility for governments to legislate and enforce rules concerning oral communication between people.

Furthermore, the Quebec Charter of Human Rights and Freedoms expressly forbids discrimination on the basis of language. No one, English or French, may be denied a job in Quebec simply because of the language he or she speaks. Cases involving this kind of discrimination in laws governing the language of work have never been tested in the courts because these laws do not violate the Charter of Human Rights and Freedoms. The legislation does not prohibit oral or written communication in English, or in any other language, between employees of a firm. Within the limits of the work they set out to accomplish, Quebecers are free to use English as their working language. And thousands do.

The provincial government has never been asked to give a clear statement on the right to work in English in Quebec. For the moment, there is no need for one; the right is there, and Quebecers have plenty of room to exercise it. If the government did attempt to go further, it would discover that its current efforts to francize the workplace probably go even now beyond the powers conferred on it by its own legislation.[87]

This situation is not widely understood by the English community. The young are particularly discouraged, and the growing loss of high school and college graduates to other provinces and the United States is the inevitable consequence.

There is no more important task facing the English than to create a climate where young English Quebecers *believe* that they have a future in Quebec and to provide help to make this belief a reality. They must first of all be convinced that, if they are bilingual, they will face no discrimination in hiring simply because their surname or first language is English. They must also be shown that, if they speak only English, they are welcome to work in jobs that require only the use of that language.

The Montreal Board of Trade could play an important role in this task. Once devoted entirely to the interests of the English business community, it has, in recent years, become an organization that works in a wider framework. However, it remains officially bilingual and does not hesitate to announce publicly that it supports a bilingual business community in Montreal. There is nothing to prevent the board from developing programs, in conjunction with its member companies, that inform young English Quebecers of the advantages of staying and working in Quebec and provide them with more opportunities to do so.

Although this will not address the problem in regions outside the Montreal area, it could well inspire initiatives in other centres.

Whatever institution makes the move—the Montreal Board of Trade, Alliance Quebec, or another group—some concrete steps must be taken, now, to reverse the flow of young English-speakers from Quebec. They must be shown that they can get or create useful and interesting jobs in their own province, and that they can work in English as well as in French.

Speaking Two Languages

The second advantage that the English community can give itself in attaining more space and power in Quebec is to make a commitment to a high level of bilingualism. Although each individual's right to a personal language policy should be respected, many have come to the conclusion that, if one chooses to live and work in Quebec, one should take advantage of the exceptional opportunities that exist to become bilingual.

The evidence that Quebecers need *both* languages is so overwhelming that it is slightly embarrassing to restate it. Bilingualism is an obvious enrichment to one's private life. Furthermore, it is a highly desirable, and in many cases essential, communications tool for success in one's work. To work in Quebec, one needs to speak French to communicate with 83 percent of the population. On the other hand, one needs to speak English because it is the principal language of the rest of Canada and of the United States, and "broken English" is the common language of the world economy.

People who are bilingual get better jobs and earn more.

Therefore, because of the generally negative attitude of French Quebec to bilingualism, it can provide English-speakers with an added economic advantage. The level of bilingualism is already significantly higher among English than among French Quebecers. As a result, the English community already has relatively more candidates available for the many jobs that require a knowledge of both languages. Over half of the English-speaking population of Quebec is now both "francophone" and "anglophone."

English Quebecers can become fluent in French as easily and as inexpensively as they can learn to add and subtract. They need not fear that they or their children will lose their first language if they learn a second one. The English community would be strengthened, not weakened, if every one of its members spoke French.

Territories

The English community should begin to think in terms of its territorial base within Quebec. For champions of individual liberties, this idea will not come easily. They tend to see the right to live in English as belonging to each person in the same degree, as being as applicable to the only English-speaking resident of a village in Beauce as to the mayor of Westmount.

Before the signs law was adopted in December 1988, a number of territorial solutions to this problem were informally tested by the government. They were all immediately rejected by the leadership of Alliance Quebec and by other leaders of the English community. In that case the rejection was understandable. But in other instances a territorial solution to certain language issues may be the best one. If we are to accept the struggle for space and power on the collective terms set by the majority, then we had better think about concentrating our limited resources in areas where the chances of success are greatest.

This need not send a message to English Quebecers in other regions that they are being abandoned. If the English community cannot maintain and increase its presence where it is already numerically strong, it will not be able to provide any real support for the rights of an isolated English resident in a village in *La Mauricie.*

A territorial approach brings important psychological benefits. It will allow the English to see themselves as exercising some real influence in at least a part of the province. It permits and encourages all kinds of local initiatives, a strengthening of local institutions, and political action. It will enable English Quebecers to say to themselves and to others that a part of the province, at least, is mainly English.

A territorial approach to the English community in Quebec does not involve a denial of individual rights. It is the logical extension of these rights into practical collective action. It does not mean that English Quebec is creating a ghetto for itself, any more than Quebec is a ghetto within Canada or North America.

Territorial rights have, in fact, existed in the language laws since they were first adopted, in the form of special rules for municipalities with English majorities. While the details of these provisions leave much to be desired, they have been generally accepted and defended by English Quebec.

Where would these "English" territories be? The precise configuration would have to be worked out with great care. They could vary according to the issues that were to be addressed.

The largest numbers of English Quebecers live close to the Ontario and the United States borders, in a belt running from the Aylmer–Buckingham area along the Ottawa River, through western and central Montreal, and into the Eastern Townships. There is also a high proportion of English Quebecers in a number of communities on the lower north shore of the St. Lawrence River.

For political purposes, the English are in the majority in five provincial ridings in the west end of Montreal, four of which are now represented by the Equality Party. There are a further five Quebec ridings in which the majority is not French-speaking, all of them on the island of Montreal. And there are important English minorities in many other electoral districts throughout the province.[88]

At the municipal level there are over 100 communities out of a total of 1,500 (14 of them in the Montreal area) where the English are in the majority.[89] A few examples of these are Aylmer, Lennoxville, and Huntingdon, all of which already have a well-established English-language infrastructure.

Many possibilities present themselves. The best place to start is in the city of Montreal.

Montreal

Like many other large cities of the world, the cultural, linguistic, and ethnic composition of Montreal is unlike that of the surrounding area. And as is the case in these other cities, the differences are going to become greater.

An examination of population statistics reveals that the English are presently a far more important factor in Montreal than in the rest of the province.

Percentage of Population by Language, 1986 [90]

	Province of Quebec		Montreal		Montreal Region	
	MT	HL	MT	HL	MT	HL
French	83	83	69	70	70	70
English	10	12	13	16	17	21
Other	7	5	18	14	13	10
Total	100	100	100	100	100	100

MT=Mother tongue   HL=Home language

In the central area of Montreal French-speaking residents are in the minority,[91] and with the added influence of tourists and business visitors, the life of downtown Montreal is, to all intents and purposes, bilingual—the wording on signs notwithstanding.

English Quebecers should make sure it stays that way, and they may find they have some allies in this project. The authorities of both the city and the Montreal Urban Community are keenly aware that Montreal's reputation as a city of international importance and its economic prosperity depend on an open, even a positive, approach to the use of English. This can be seen clearly in the promotional material prepared by them for use outside the province. While stating that Quebec is mainly French, it emphasizes the possibilities for living there in English. Jobs, construction, and taxes all depend on this approach.

The provincial government is no less unequivocal. The bilingual character of Montreal is stressed to potential investors and to the international financial community. Quebec's minister of international affairs was only repeating what has been said many times before when he recently told the Canadian Business Club in Seoul, South Korea, that

> Montreal is probably the only truly bilingual city in the world. . . . This linguistic duality has allowed us to keep very close ties with Europe, whether it be France or England. So I sincerely believe that in an age of globalization, the intimate knowledge of two languages and the non-artificial presence of two strong cultures is a definite asset for Quebec. And never mind what some of our critics say, I can tell you that our business people are very happy to be able to conduct business in the United States or in France with the same ease.[92]

In other words, outside the province, the municipal and provincial governments are already saying that Quebec, or at least Montreal, is bilingual.

Many key sectors of the Montreal economy require the use of

113

the English language. For instance, the aerospace, pharmaceutical, and electronics companies, the financial institutions, and the infrastructure that supports them in Montreal can only remain and grow there if agreement exists on the use of English as well as French in the workplace.

There are already many points of contact between English and French business and community leaders in Montreal. Every effort should be made to develop a consensus on the affirmation of Montreal as the bilingual city it already is, one that is promoted and recognized as such throughout the world. There are a number of French-speaking Quebecers who would not be unsympathetic to this notion of using the truth as a tool for advancing the prosperity of everyone. The message that Quebec, particularly Montreal, is open and welcoming to people who speak English and wish to live here in that language is essential to the economic prosperity of the province.

The development of Montreal, which must compete with other urban areas in Canada and the United States, requires a concerted effort by the whole community. If it is to be developed only in French, then only the French-speaking leadership will be encouraged to contribute. If it is developed as a bilingual city, the entire community will be able to identify with it and participate in its development.

Immigration

Acting on W.C. Fields's premise that "anybody who hates children can't be all bad," the English in Quebec are reproducing themselves with no more enthusiasm than are the French.[93] This means that if the English community is to grow, to at least recover its losses of the past fifteen years, much of the increase will have to come from immigration or from linguistic transfers by people who are already here.

English Quebecers have always been among the most mobile of Canadians. Many leave for extended periods and eventually return. The current problem is that more are leaving, and fewer are coming back.

This trend, like any other, is reversible. Even if we were to set for ourselves a long-term objective of 20 percent of the population we would certainly not be posing any threat to the remaining 80 percent who would be French-speaking. More realistically, we might think, as a specific goal, of rebuilding our numbers to where they were in absolute terms in 1976, which would require an increase of about 120,000—from 680,000 to 800,000. Doing so would ensure the numbers necessary to maintain and develop English institutions. Most important, having growth as a goal would in itself create a new sense of optimism and purpose.

We should encourage more English-speaking people to move to Quebec. The best place to start is with English-speaking people from the rest of Canada, because they do not require a visa.

The English community in Quebec has spent the last fifteen years in an understandable state of schizophrenia on the subject of life for an English person here. In a sense we have been our own worst enemies. French-speaking Quebecers are frequently upset by negative reports in the media outside the province, which claim that they are inhospitable to the English. The English should be even more upset, because every report of this kind makes Quebec a little less appealing to the very people needed to strengthen our community.

The time has come to pass a clear message to English-speaking people outside the province: life is good in Quebec, and they can live here in English if they want to. They should be assured that they will be supported by a strong and confident community. They will have the opportunity to learn French, and so will their children. This advantage will permit them not only to live more fully in Quebec, but also to move more freely in a changing world and to understand themselves and their neighbours in a new and better way. But we will remind them that no one will oblige them to speak French and that they

115

will find that they can live in English if that is what they want to do.

Promoting Quebec to the English outside the province should not be difficult. It is one of the best places in North America to live—the place is beautiful, the infrastructure excellent. When one considers the aspects of collective life that concern most people—health care, educational facilities, crime rates and police protection, the cost of living, tax rates, the quality of municipal services, labour relations, the transportation system, recreational facilities, cultural diversity, access to other regions, the justice system, opportunities for growth and economic prosperity—Quebecers can say without fear of contradiction that their province is among the truly desirable places to live. People who come to Quebec to see for themselves confirm it every day.

For an English Quebecer, the fact that 83 percent of the population speaks French is not a problem. Let it be said again that French is an advantage, an additional benefit available to English Quebecers and their children, which no one can impose on them but which will enrich their lives if they grasp it. If we believe this ourselves, we can convince others.

English Quebec also has a positive message to pass on to immigrants whose first language is neither French nor English. The English-language community described in this book is not defined by ethnic origin, country of birth, colour, or religion. It is made up, simply, of those who wish to live in Quebec primarily in the English language.

Each year, there is a growing number of immigrants to Quebec whose first language is neither English nor French. In 1989 they numbered 34,000, and 89 percent of them settled in Montreal. Thirty-four percent spoke English as a second language when they arrived.[94] In other words, a third of all immigrants should be able to integrate rather easily into the English community if that is their wish.

One of the central preoccupations of the provincial government is to ensure that these newly arrived citizens become integrated into Quebec society. If, by this, the government means that new Quebecers should learn French and feel at home with the province's institutions, then the English would certainly support this policy. But if the government proposes to discourage immigrants from learning or using English, then we cannot agree.

If we believe that bilingualism is a valuable asset for our own economic and cultural well-being, then we cannot send a message to immigrants that the only language they need to understand is French. It is unlikely that they would believe us in any event. They would certainly not respect us for saying one thing to those who were already in the province and another to those who had just arrived.

New immigrants are aware that they are coming to a country whose government has two official languages, a province whose government has one, and two charters of human rights that sanction all tongues. In Quebec, we expect that the state will try to ensure that all newcomers learn to speak French fluently and explain the advantages of integrating into the French community. The English community should accept the responsibility for explaining the advantages of Quebec's alternative language.

After that, new Quebecers deserve our respect for their capacity and their right to choose the language (or languages) they prefer, free from all coercion. Our success in persuading immigrants to integrate into our community will depend on how appealing and open we are able to make it, on how warmly we welcome the stranger in our midst.

There is more than one way to fit into the diverse life of Quebec. *Any* immigrant, regardless of where he or she comes from, can join the English community of Quebec and still be a "real" Quebecer.

ORGANIZING FOR CHANGE

. . . and all things thought upon
That may with reasonable swiftness add
More feathers to our wings.

Henry V
Act I, scene ii

Institutions

If the English are to grow and contribute to Quebec life as they have in the past, it will require collective as well as individual effort. This collective energy must find its outlet in more than cheerleading. The community's institutions must be made stronger.

Many of Quebec's institutions are not language-based. They involve both English- and French-speaking people, working together. Because the two linguistic groups are so close in Quebec, physically and in their interests and activities, it is both inevitable and highly useful that much of the institutional framework should be shared. English and French Quebecers work in the same businesses, use the same stores, travel together, and participate in an increasing number of community organizations. Until recently, most of them voted for the same political parties.

However, they have separate institutions as well. English and French are normally attracted to their own news media, schools, health care and social service bodies, churches, and charitable organizations. There are even institutions in Quebec whose only objective is to foster the interests of a particular language group. The French have had such organizations for years. The English-language counterparts are more recent, with Alliance Quebec being the most important but not the only example.

The English community's institutions can be organized into four groups:

— Language-based groups, such as Alliance Quebec

— Organizations that deliver specific services, such as schools and hospitals

— Cultural institutions, such as the press, the electronic media, and the arts

— Political parties

All of these institutions are essential in maintaining and expanding the English community.

Language-Based Groups

The strategies so far proposed for the English community do not require political action. No one need go to Quebec City to make them happen. They are essentially personal initiatives. They will, however, require an organized community effort to succeed.

Alliance Quebec is the organization in which these activities can be most easily defined, financed, and carried out, and it is important to examine the recent history of the institution that has come to be recognized as the official voice of English Quebec.

The Alliance has about ten thousand individual members and is also a federation of regional voluntary groups and organizations. It has an elected board of directors, and its president is recognized as the principal spokesperson for the English community. With about fifteen full-time employees and a budget of $1,500,000, it is funded primarily by the federal government under its program for the promotion of minority linguistic groups across Canada. Since its creation, Alliance Quebec has performed a number of functions in its role as the ultimate voice of the English-speaking community:

POLICY-MAKING Its structures have encouraged the development of plans and programs to strengthen the English community and its institutions. The Liberal Party program for the English and the amendments to Bill 101 made by the Parti Québécois government in 1983 were both inspired by studies and resolutions of the Alliance.

PROVIDING INFORMATION It conducts research projects and serves as a resource centre for the English-speaking community.

PROVIDING PERSONAL ASSISTANCE It provides help to individuals and organizations who find themselves in difficulty as a result of Quebec's language legislation. It has arranged for legal advice and financing to enable test cases to be brought before the courts.

LOBBYING It lobbies the provincial government with briefs, personal contacts, and public declarations on legislative matters affecting the interests of its members. It also spends considerable time lobbying the federal government and the governments of the other provinces on questions of interest to all of Canada's linguistic minorities.

BRIDGE BUILDING Its leaders make regular efforts to maintain a public and private dialogue with leaders of the French community in an effort to strengthen relationships and create greater understanding between the two groups.

TRAINING It has stimulated many members of the English community to a greater awareness and involvement in public life in Quebec. Former employees and directors of the Alliance occupy some of the most important government posts held by members of the English community.[95]

The most visible part of all this activity has been political lobbying, and the recent results have not been outstanding. In 1985 the Alliance was in the public mind closely linked to the Liberal program for the English community. The government's subsequent refusal to implement that program, which culminated in the signs debate, prompted a number of observers to question whether there was any point to the continued existence of Alliance Quebec.

But reports of its death were premature. In the 1989 election the Alliance broke publicly with the Liberals and urged English voters *not* to vote for that party. This was a gamble, but it paid off when the majority of English voters followed that advice, and as a result the Alliance's credibility as a legitimate voice of the community was reinforced.

This rather daring excursion into partisan politics was successful, but under ordinary circumstances it should probably not be repeated. It need not be, because the Alliance has an extremely important role to play in activities that do not require action or even approval by any government or political party.

The Alliance's present activities can be summarized in two main goals: to *help* the English community's members and institutions, and to *represent* that community to the French-speaking majority and the governments of Quebec and Canada. The Alliance might now wish to consider the advisability of an expansion of the activities associated with the first goal and a little less emphasis on activities associated with the second. For instance, each of the projects proposed earlier for English Quebecers should be reinforced by programs of the Alliance. Each will require a continuing effort, carefully organized and adequately financed. These activities can be grouped around one central idea: *the expansion in Quebec of the English language and the English-language community.*

The emphasis here is on "expansion." The goal of replacing the 120,000 English Quebecers who have been lost to the community since 1976 could very well be the Alliance's principal mandate for the next decade. By adopting it, the Alliance would reduce its dependence on political parties and governments for its success. It would take the future of the community into its own hands and embark on programs whose success does not depend solely on the support of the French-speaking majority. It would put itself on a playing field on which it has a reasonable chance of emerging a winner.

Concretely, activities relating to policy formulation and the provision of information and assistance would be expanded. In addition, the Alliance would undertake a series of programs to expand the use of English in Quebec. It could:

— sponsor a public campaign to encourage the greater use of English by members of the community in their capacity as consumers and workers.

123

— organize English-language courses and other activities to welcome immigrants of all ethnic origins into the English-speaking community.

— develop a public relations program aimed at the rest of Canada to improve Quebec's image as a place to live in English.

— find further ways to improve the availability of French-language courses, which are not now publicly financed, for adults whose first language is English.

— in collaboration with organizations such as the Montreal Board of Trade, or alone, begin programs to keep young English Quebecers in Quebec after they finish their education.

— continue and expand its interest in strengthening the artistic and intellectual resources of the English community.

Some of these programs might be financed by the federal government within the framework of its minority-language activities. However, additional and continuing financial support would be required from the English community. It will cost money to ensure the future of English Quebec, and new ways of funding will have to be developed within the community. The English would respond positively to this appeal if it was presented as the only way to secure the future of English-language institutions— which it is.

This new orientation does not mean that the Alliance should end its lobbying efforts or that it should avoid taking a public stand on political issues that affect the English. If it is to remain credible as the voice of the community, it must have well-developed positions on political issues and state them. But the success of the organization should no longer be measured primarily by these activities and their results. The Alliance must be successful, and the possibilities for regular success in the political arena at the present time are too remote.

The Alliance has a key role to play and important things to do within its own community, outside the realm of politics. In these activities, the possibilities of success lie within the community's own hands. The English of Quebec have a pressing need to see themselves in a positive way—as winners, as a group whose members have unrivalled opportunities for success in Quebec, Canada, and North America, *because* they are English Quebecers. They need to be shown that they can carry on the long tradition of service and contribution to the larger Quebec community in their own language.

Alliance Quebec can be a catalyst for creating this climate. It will succeed, not by endless debates on television with representatives of the Société Saint-Jean-Baptiste, but by enlarging the membership of the English community and by finding new strengths and new resources internally.

This new orientation will make it easy to find leadership for Alliance Quebec. Those who hesitate, for very practical reasons, to be seen as spokespeople for an organization that is constantly in opposition to the government will be reassured. On a more idealistic plane, it will be a pleasure and a challenge to spend one's time strengthening a community so that it can be of greater benefit both to its own members and to all of Quebec.

Service Organizations

Not much more will be said here about English Quebec's service-based organizations. The English community's involvement in them has always been at a high level, and the structures that permit this have been in place for a long time.

The most important of these institutions, those in the educational and health and social service sectors, are financed by the provincial government. As a result, their policy and administration are extensively controlled, and some of their problems are really political matters. Many of these political issues are not only language-related; they are the result of financial and administrative constraints shared by the whole system.

The main point is that the English have created, and continue to involve themselves in an impressive way in, a very wide range of service institutions. The school commissions and hospital boards of directors are supplemented by numerous organizations representing their users and employees. They form the essential framework that supports the whole community. Their leaders should have no hesitation about affirming, and insisting on, the essentially English character of these vital institutions.

Cultural Institutions

It is vital that we remind ourselves of the importance of our cultural institutions. If we are still here it is because we have found ways to talk about ourselves, to rethink and redefine our identity. This has not been accomplished by lone individuals but in dialogue, on English-language radio and TV stations, in newspapers, and at meetings of numerous and diverse English-language organizations and associations.

In books going as far back as *Two Solitudes,* in plays like *Balconville,* an editorial in the *Gazette,* or a meeting of the Home and School Association in Aylmer we glue ourselves more firmly together by reflection and debate on what we are and what we might become. Our cultural resources are extensive, but one has the impression that we have not spent much time thinking about these resources as a whole, or about ways to broaden them.[96]

A great deal of the culture of the English Quebecer is Canadian or American. We see ourselves reflected in the CBC and CBS, in *Maclean's* and *Time,* and in all the other cultural institutions of the worldwide English community.

We contribute to this wider culture, too. A moment's reflection is enough to realize that there is no one place in Canada that makes the CBC what it is and no unique spot in the United

States that perfectly represents the American way of life. Our own ideas, and the artists who bring them to life, are ingredients in the recipe, as are the consumers of the resulting menu. Bruce Springsteen is not from "America" but from New Jersey; Oscar Peterson is from Montreal.

However, our own special flavour becomes more pronounced when the dish is prepared in smaller quantities, and activities that originate in English Quebec for consumption by our own community are an essential element in a balanced cultural diet. At this local level there are some aspects of our culture that, by definition, surpass linguistic boundaries. The visual arts, music, and spectator sports are three examples. Here the question of whether one is English or French is irrelevant, and the whole community can work together to achieve something of value.

But other local cultural institutions must be language-based. One group of these is centred around our educational institutions and especially the universities and CEGEPs. Apart from their role in formal education, they provide a wealth of facilities for the community. Their buildings, libraries, theatres, stadiums, and auditoriums are used by us all. More important, the faculties of these institutions are an important resource for reflection on the community. Members of the faculties of McGill, Concordia, Bishop's, John Abbott, Champlain, Heritage, and Dawson contribute enormously to the advancement of English Quebec studies and to the current debate on public affairs—and one has the impression that we have not yet fully realized the potential of these resources.

A second, and very rich, cultural base is found in our community associations, such as churches, farmers' groups, literary societies, theatre groups, Women's Institutes, and amateur sports organizations. We have been instrumental in the foundation and funding of a number of highly useful institutions, including the YMCA and YWCA, public libraries, and homes for the elderly. Many of these organizations serve specific religious and ethnic groups within the larger community.

The communications media are the most visible and powerful

part of the cultural structures that bind our community together. English Quebec has ten private radio stations and one private TV outlet. Furthermore, the CBC maintains a system of AM and FM radio and television, most of which originates in Montreal but is generally available throughout the province. There are two daily newspapers and about fifteen community-based weeklies. So the voice of English Quebec can be heard with relative ease today by us all.

During the past decade the English-language media—notably the Montreal *Gazette*, the two English TV stations, the English radio network of the CBC, and radio stations CJAD and CFCF— have quite literally kept the community alive by providing a daily forum in which the English have talked over their problems and reassured themselves about their possibilities in the future.

This summary is only a brief inventory of English Quebec's cultural institutions, made to remind readers of their crucial importance in our future. How to keep them and make them stronger, how to develop new ones, how to contribute to the wider culture of Quebec and the world—posing these questions and seeking the answers is a vital part of the process of strengthening the English community and making it more interesting.

Political Institutions

Many projects for the English community do not require the support of the provincial authorities. But there are others that are subject to government legislation or intervention, and for this reason the political orientation of the community is very important. When political parties ask the English for our support, we should be prepared to tell them what we ask in return.

The first request, on which all the others depend, is the matter of formal recognition. The English community is a distinct society in Quebec. It has a right to recognition as such, and to the support and encouragement of the provincial and federal governments in a way that will permit us to remain, to grow, and to develop in our own way.

There are two language communities here. This should be specifically recognized in the laws of Quebec. We seek the "open and explicit legal recognition" that was first promised by the leader of the Liberal Party of Quebec in 1978. Most members of the English community share their government's intention to encourage the widespread use of the French language. They have demonstrated that they want to participate in that expansion by encouraging bilingualism in their own community, over half of which now speaks French.

The English community accepts the idea that one should be able to live fully in the French language in Quebec. But it opposes official gestures that do not demonstrably further this objective, gestures that are simply designed to reduce the space occupied by the English community, to show who is "boss," or to impose an official culture. The English community wishes to be considered explicitly by its government as an asset to Quebec. The English will support political parties that are prepared to endorse this view and its consequences.

What are some of the consequences? The first that springs to mind, because it is so fresh in the memory, is related to the question of signs. The English community can never accept that the visible face of Quebec should be exclusively French. Quebec is French and English or, quite acceptably, FRENCH and English, and that reality must be given visible expression.

No one has even begun to demonstrate that the future of the French language is threatened by English on signs or that, with the adoption of Bill 178, French has been made more secure. English signs have been present in Quebec for two centuries, and the French community has grown stronger during this period. The law was adopted to satisfy the most unacceptable forces of linguistic nationalism. In the words of Richard French, "the argument for French unilingualism is without empirical foundation and rests on a flagrant misuse of the notion

129

of collective rights."[97] It is as unacceptable today as it was when first adopted.

The public school system should be restructured in a way that allows *all* English-speaking people to send their children to English-language schools. This is not a fundamental right—the state can organize its educational system in any way that it sees fit—but the idea that the English system should be available to all English-speaking people is as valid now as it was when proposed by the Liberal Party in 1978.

The English are mobile, and in the years ahead, in a common market with the United States, there will be even more movement between Quebec, its southern neighbour, and other English-speaking areas of the world. The present system, with its special permits for those on a "temporary" stay (of up to ten years!) is unfair to all except the elite.

The English community has a right to be cared for, to be sick, and to grow old, in English. In areas with English populations, the health and social service institutions should offer full services in English. The law adopted a few years ago, which was supposed to ensure this, needs to be implemented, and continuing financial resources should be committed to it.

The entire Quebec health system is now being reviewed to make it more effective and its institutional structures less cumbersome. This is a critical period for the future of English-language health and social services.[98] If the law is to provide only one system for both English and French, then within this system, English services should be available for all who require them. If these guarantees cannot be given and supported by the necessary funding, the English should be provided with specifically English-language services, with institutional structures similar to those in the educational system.

There are other cases in which English Quebec's institutions should more fully reflect the diversity of the community in which they are located. One of these is municipal government. Quebec's largest city, Montreal, is 13 percent English-speaking. A number of municipalities, including some in the Montreal region, have an English majority, and many more have significant English minorities. They should be required to provide their services in English as well as French.

In 1972 the Gendron Report on the status of the French language proposed that communities in which 10 percent of the population was English-speaking should publish their documents in both languages—a rule similar to the one in effect in Finland with respect to its Swedish minority.[99] However, the Charter of the French language requires the English to make up over 50 percent of a community's population before they have the right to municipal services in their own language.[100]

In other words, under Quebec law the English must be in the *majority* in their community to have the right to services that would normally be accorded to a significant minority. Furthermore, the drop from 50 percent to 49 percent in a community that has the right to use the English language apparently results in a cancellation of that right.[101] It is difficult to imagine a more unfair delineation of minority rights than this.

There are now about one hundred municipalities in which the majority of the population is English-speaking.[102] A number of these—for example, Roxboro, Pierrefonds, Mount Royal, Sutton, and Stanstead—could lose their right to English services in the near future.

A total of 283 of Quebec's fifteen hundred municipalities have English minorities of over 10 percent. It is difficult to understand a principle of collective rights that denies these minorities the right to services in their own language from the authorities to whom they pay their taxes. The right to civilized minority-language rights in Quebec's municipalities should become a major political objective of English Quebec. It should be extended not only to the English, but to those who speak other languages as well.

The need for a strong English presence in government institutions that offer services to the public is easy to demonstrate. Nevertheless, the promises of successive governments to increase the participation of English Quebecers in the civil service have not been respected.

English Quebecers have the same complaints about the provincial bureaucracy that French Quebecers had about Ottawa twenty years ago. However, we do not require a civil service that functions internally in two languages. What we do need is a means by which any individual or organization can address its government in English and get an answer in that language.

Quebec needs enough people in the public service whose first language is English to enable English Quebecers to identify easily with their own government. Achieving this will demand more than the declarations of intent to which all have become accustomed. It requires a program to make it happen, with periodic and public disclosure of progress, by an independent body.

In passing, there is another worthwhile, if long-term, political project to be mentioned: a close examination of the idea of introducing proportional representation into the Quebec legislature. Already an established feature of many European states, it is a civilized way to ensure real representation of all the significant elements in a diverse society, elements seldom found within narrow geographical boundaries. It can make life more difficult for governments, but it enhances the role of each elected member of the legislature. Some of the most politically stable democracies in the world use it with success. If adopted in Quebec, proportional representation would permit the establishment of a real voice for the English community (and other important interests) in the politics of the province.

Political Parties

Most of the political objectives outlined above have been voiced many times in the past. As someone said about the menu at the Savoy Hotel, "There is nothing here that a reasonable man could refuse." They all devolve quite naturally from the idea of a fully recognized English Quebec that is given space to grow and contribute to the welfare of all, without in any way impinging on the rights of the majority of Quebecers to live and work in French.

However, between the fancy and the fact lie some formidable obstacles. At present there appears to be no political party in Quebec that could endorse such a program for the English community and then win an election to implement it. The search for a solution to this problem, through support of a broadly based organization such as the Liberal Party of Quebec or a group with more limited objectives, such as the Equality Party—or both of them—is one of the more stimulating challenges now facing the community.

Immediately after the adoption of the signs law in December 1988, the idea that the English community could have political influence seemed as hopeless as the idea of a "community of English Quebecers" had been only a few years earlier. Fifteen years of work within the Liberal Party had produced almost no result.

The elections in December 1989 made everyone think again. For the first time in the history of Quebec, a party that represented nothing but the English-speaking community was brought into being. In the ridings where it was possible to do so, two-thirds of the English community voted for it, and four of its candidates were elected.

Some said that this was simply a protest vote against the signs law, a knee-jerk reaction that would disappear as quickly as it had arrived. They argued that a "one-issue" political party in a parliamentary system of government is not really a party at all and that, if very few of English Quebec's political goals were realized within the framework of the Liberal Party, then a minority party such as this could never realize any of them. They would probably add that the Equality Party's performance since the election has fallen somewhat short of brilliance. Perhaps so; but a little further analysis is justified in the face of these unprecedented events.

First, it is possible that the Equality Party, despite the special circumstances that gave it birth, is in fact the logical, even inevitable, consequence of the emergence of the real sense of commu-

133

nity among the English of Quebec that began almost fifteen years ago. If the English do exist as a community, and if many decisions vital to its future are to be decided in the National Assembly, then what is more natural for it than to seek a political voice that clearly expresses its views?

Admittedly, the English are a small minority in Quebec, an English party will always be a minority party, and every effort to broaden its base will result in some dilution of its original idea. But between the "rainbow coalition" that the Liberal Party of Quebec has become and a single-issue political formation, there is ample space to use some imagination.

To hold power, the Liberal Party has assembled a coalition of voters from the business and rural communities who are traditionally among the most conservative elements of Quebec society. Their numbers are reinforced, for the time being at least, by people of all ideological persuasions who will not vote for a separatist party, regardless of how they feel about any other issues.

For the past fifty years the English of Quebec have also identified with and voted for the Liberal Party. But the Liberal Party has now left the English community, in a sense that goes beyond the signs issue and to the very heart of the party's electoral calculations. It appears that, as a result, many members of the English community have, temporarily at least, left the Liberal Party.

Will they return? Many of them are, by tradition, liberals, but the question of political ideology scarcely enters into the question anymore. "Liberalism" has meant different things at different times.[103] The present Liberal Party and its government spend very little time torturing themselves over their purity in any event. If liberalism means "change" or "reform," few could argue that the past five years have been liberal years. If it means devotion to *individual rights,* the record speaks for itself.

From now on, the English will be just one of a number of groups that exercise pressure on the Liberal Party of Quebec. It seems highly unlikely that very many serious internal debates touching on language issues will be settled in their favour. In the meantime, as the community's influence in the Liberal Party has been declining, its awareness of itself as a group with common objectives has grown dramatically. It can now be mobilized for a number of activities, including political action. The English now have an alternative, that of strengthening, and continuing to vote for, their own political party.

The English vote in Quebec is still important, and the total vote of all those who are not French is even more so. There is political strength here that merits attention by the political strategists of all parties. The vote of people of other ethnic origins, such as Italian, Greek, or Portuguese, cannot be taken for granted by either the English or the French, or by any political party. However, it seems that, like the English, many of these citizens do not instinctively share some of the narrower definitions of Quebec nationalism that are currently on offer.

The following table is a breakdown of the linguistic composition of the 125 counties represented in the National Assembly of Quebec. Totals for those who are English and for those whose first language is not French are shown separately.

The Importance of the Non-Francophone Vote in Quebec[104]

Share of Non-French Vote	Number of Counties	
	English Mother Tongue	Non-French Mother Tongue
Over 50%	5	10
40–49%	7	16
30–39%	10	22
20–29%	18	32
10–19%	30	50
5–9%	53	73
0–4%	72	52

To put the numbers into words, there are five ridings in Quebec that have an English-speaking majority and ten that have a majority other than French. Of the 125 counties, fifty have linguistic minorities of over 10 percent. Considering that 10 percent of the voting population in a county comprises about 3,500 persons and that about half of the counties in Quebec gave victory margins of less than this amount in the 1989 elections, it is clear that the non-French vote in Quebec can be very important.

Good arguments in favour of supporting the Liberal Party remain. Most importantly, that party is the one in power, and no English-based organization will ever be able to make that claim. The Liberal Party still has an important number of English members, and it would be unfair to suggest that they are without influence or that all the party's French-speaking members are deaf to the aspirations of their English-speaking colleagues. Some English Quebecers will wish to work from within, in the hope that they can convince the party to change its policies and at least respect the commitments it made in 1985.

On the other hand, by supporting the Equality Party the English need not fear that they will be without influence in the political decision-making process. Any government, for practical reasons, will seek to represent all significant elements in society. The present government's weakness in certain areas—for instance, in the Saguenay area or with the labour union movement—does not mean that those elements of society are ignored. It is possible to argue that, like "prodigal sons," they receive more support and attention than if they were loyal members of the family. At present the English are represented in the Liberal government and have their own party as well.

So the Equality Party and the majority of the English community that supported it have some heavy responsibilities and some difficult choices to make in the months ahead. The party has not increased its credibility or broadened its base, even in the English community, during the first two years of its existence.

One possibility is that the party will simply disappear, having been only the temporary manifestation of an explosion of discontent over a single issue. However, this is not inevitable. It is quite possible that provided the elected members of the Equality Party continue to represent the concerns of their electors, they would be re-elected. Voters, like everyone else, like to feel they made the right decision. For this same reason the Equality Party might continue to attract the important support it obtained from English voters in about fifteen other ridings in 1989.

The English community might also consider strengthening the leadership and broadening the base of the Equality Party by adopting policies that appeal to other groups. Other minority linguistic groups represent a particularly fertile opportunity. They are growing in numbers, and their instinctive association with the Liberal Party is not reinforced by the insistence that they should learn and speak French, and only French, if they want to be considered "good" Quebecers.

The lack of enthusiasm with which some senior members of the Quebec Liberal Party perceive the Canadian federation also represents an important opportunity for the Equality Party, not only with minority linguistic groups but with a number of French-speaking Quebecers as well. There are over fifty provincial ridings, along the borders of Ontario and the United States and in western and central Montreal, where the loyalty of a large portion of the population to the Canadian federation remains very powerful.

When writing its program, the Equality Party, all considerations of language and the constitution aside, might examine the possibility that a "liberal" party, one with the human being at the centre, might attract a surprisingly large number of fellow citizens, including French. The Liberal Party of Quebec cannot fill this role in the forseeable future. The nationalist and collectivist preoccupations that currently dominate Quebec life make it almost impossible for that party to think about the larger political issues, except to the extent that these issues are forced on it by interest groups demanding immediate redress.

A liberal Equality Party, devoted to seeking concrete applications of the principles of individual liberty, will not win a general election in Quebec. But an English party is not going to win one in any event. It could, however, render a real service, and perhaps even win a number of votes among other language groups, by reminding all Quebecers of the possibilities for individual and collective fulfilment in a society based, not on nationalism and pressure-group politics, but on the unending effort to free citizens from constraints on the realization of their full potential.

When it comes to the language question there will be a promising place in the years ahead for a party that clearly and uncompromisingly advocates a bilingual Quebec. Those who wish to support a party in favour of a French Quebec will continue to have ample choice. But, for many others, French as well as English, a party that insists on the advantages of bilingualism at both the personal and collective levels could have a great attraction. It would conform closely to their view of how they wished to order their own lives and those of their children. It would also conform quite closely to reality.

In other words, the Equality Party has the potential to become more than the sum of its present representatives and policies. It is already the political voice of tens of thousands of English Quebecers. It could become an interesting base for developing an alternative vision of Quebec society, one more sensitive to and in tune with the phenomenal changes taking place in the world. Furthermore, if future elections in Quebec give smaller majorities to the government (who can predict?), the English vote and the Equality Party seats in the National Assembly may acquire a level of influence that will justify the difficult period of political adolescence the party is now enduring.

The English community does have a political future in Quebec. It will never vote monolithically for a single party. Many of its members will decide that their best interests lie in the Liberal Party, where they can work for change from within; they have important work to do there. Others may choose the Parti Québécois. But the creation and the success of the Equality Party is not necessarily a passing phenomenon. It is a logical consequence of the birth of a real Quebec English community, one that has expanded and will continue to expand its institutions into every field of activity. A party representing the English community could have an important role to play in the years ahead.

Whatever party English Quebecers choose, it seems illogical that they would support any political party that does not accept, as part of its program, measures that the community deems vital for its own future. Would any other group do so?

COLLABORATION

. . . when France is mine and I am yours,
then yours is France and you are mine.

Henry V
Act V, scene ii

Cultural Insecurity

This book is written for English Quebecers. Its purpose is to suggest some things we can do, projects largely within our own control, to assure our future. But English Quebecers are not alone. By the very fact of stating our intention to remain "distinct," we recognize the existence of others in the same room. This final chapter looks again at the present social and political climate, one that is determined, not by English Quebecers, but by our French-speaking neighbours, who outnumber us by almost ten to one.

We intend to affirm ourselves and make our contribution to the life of the province as English Quebecers. It is, however, the French-speaking majority that will decide whether these goals will be accomplished in a spirit of confrontation or of collaboration. It appears that the choice they make will depend essentially on how they perceive what has come to be known as their "cultural security."

In a 1989 interview in which he explained the signs law to the rest of Canada, Prime Minister Brian Mulroney said that "as the French language is strengthened, [the] cultural uncertainties that give rise to this attitude [of being threatened in an overwhelmingly English-speaking North America] will diminish and hopefully be gone so that we can have the kind of minority freedoms and protections we all want."[105]

Acceptance and collaboration will, it seems, be possible when the "uncertainties" are removed and cultural security materializes. It seems pertinent to ask what this much-desired state of affairs might look like—and how, and when, it might be brought about.

Cultural Security

Today, when the political and intellectual leaders of French-speaking Quebec meditate on "the English," the prevailing mood is negative. It is based on a fear that the French community will eventually be catabolized by this powerful force. This recurring theme in the social, cultural, and political discourse of the province is as powerful today as it was two hundred years ago.

It seems almost superfluous to quote those who express this preoccupation. A few examples will suffice. Léon Dion says that

> writers here in Quebec are well aware that French is living on borrowed time and that it is gradually degenerating.[106]

Martine Corrivault, an editorialist for *Le Soleil,* advises that

> francophone Quebec is a little state, attacked on all its borders and unable even to count on a vigilant attitude on the part of francophone Europe.[107]

A recent Liberal Party program says that

> we must face up to reality: the survival of the French fact in North America is at stake.[108]

Michel Roy feels that it is essential to

> inform Canada of the reality of the dangers which face the French culture and French society in Quebec.[109]

And the federal commissioner of official languages advises that

> few informed observers could deny that the French language, which is in a minority position in Canada and still more so in North America, is seriously threatened.[110]

These are the moderate voices. The "Letters to the Editor" pages of many French-language newspapers express this feeling of insecurity daily in a much more colourful fashion. In fact, the faith of linguistic insecurity has become the closest thing we now have to a catechism. Everyone, it seems, looks forward to despair.

It is worth noting that there is no unanimity on exactly what is at stake. The statements quoted above contain references to "French," "francophone Quebec," "the French fact," "French culture," and "French society." The various expressions reflect, first of all, a concern with linguistic demography. It *is* a fact that about 5,400,000 French-speaking Quebecers are surrounded by fifty times as many English-speaking North Americans. But, beyond the arithmetic, there is also the feeling that a "culture," a way of life, is in danger of being lost.

For example, many of the writers whom Léon Dion refers to as "living on borrowed time" have their roots in a rural and Catholic Quebec, with a people in close contact with the physical environment, often underprivileged and sometimes exploited, but vibrant, wise, and family-based. Other writers are preoccupied with efforts to break out of that way of life and make sense of a new environment. Those who have managed to escape into the secular and urban world often express frustration that real economic or cultural participation in it seems difficult or impossible, except in English. The dominant theme of the Quebec writer has been described as "a subversive celebration of that limited and pathetic transcendence achieved against all the odds,"[111] as the world of the beautiful loser.

The feelings of isolation and insecurity are not confined to the artistic community. The president of the Quebec Chamber of Commerce recently declared that he is "astounded by the number of black and yellow people who live in Montreal," that these newcomers "do not form part of the reality of the Quebec people," and that he hopes to do what he can to correct the situation.[112] These remarks would have aroused a torrent of protest in many other parts of the world, but they were scarcely questioned here.

In the face of this preoccupation with keeping things as they were, the government of Quebec is faced with a dilemma. It can, within limits, legislate an official language; but, happily for all of us, there is no way for the state to legislate an official culture. In a democracy, all must be allowed to sing their own songs and to place their own values on the community's existing cultural and social traditions.

The application of this democratic ideal is turning out to be a major problem for most of the developed countries of the world, and we have not been spared. A Quebec populated by Anglo-Saxons, Italians, Haitians, and Vietnamese, by people of many religions—even if they all speak French—may well be a French Quebec. But it is not a French QUEBEC.

To complicate matters further, the present culture of French Quebec means different things to different people. The French themselves have been disloyal to their own culture, if one compares today's society in Quebec with that of the 1950s and before. Léon Dion laments this transformation:

> More often than not, change involved scrapping traditional values with little thought for what might replace them or whether such values were even available, at home or abroad. . . .

and

> Few people, at least until recently, have stopped to wonder what has become of the sense of the sacred in Quebec. It has, unfortunately, all but disappeared: young people, in particular, search in vain for values to shape their personal development and end up looking elsewhere, chiefly to the United States.[113]

In the face of such passionate rhetoric, one might imagine that the French community and the use of French language are declining in Quebec. It is evident that the community no longer resembles the one that Mr. Dion holds dear. But the proposition that the French-language community in Quebec is becoming weaker is not supported by either quantitative analysis or casual observation. Exactly the opposite is happening.

145

English-speaking people in Quebec have never represented more than a small minority. At their peak in 1861, they represented 24 percent of the population.[114] One hundred years later, in 1961, the figure had declined to 14 percent. By 1986, the most recent date for which figures are available, it was down to 10 percent.

By any measure, the dominance of the French by the English is a myth. In terms of relative incomes there has been a spectacular change. In 1961 the average English Quebecer earned 51 percent more than a French Quebecer. In 1971 the difference was 33 percent; in 1980 it was down to 14 percent;[115] and it is reasonable to assume that today there is no difference at all. The English and French of Quebec are today either equally rich or equally poor.

Until the 1970s, immigrants to Quebec had traditionally integrated into the English educational system. In recent years this practice has changed dramatically; the proportion of immigrants attending French schools rose from 23 percent to 65 percent between 1978 and 1988.[116]

A perennial complaint of French-speaking Quebecers is their inability to be served in their own language in commercial establishments in Montreal. A recent study by the Council of the French Language[117] reveals that service in French is now available in over 90 percent of all establishments, including those in the English, Italian, and Chinese quarters of the city. In the past twenty years the possibility of living, working, and playing in French in Montreal, as elsewhere in the province, has greatly increased. It is not inaccurate to say that a province that was 70 percent French has become 85 percent French.

Has this given the French-speaking community more confidence in itself and reduced the "cultural uncertainties" to which Brian Mulroney referred? Apparently not. The prevailing sentiment, officially approved and even encouraged by the political leadership of the province, is that the community is threatened as never before. If a French-speaking leader was to suggest publicly, employing the arguments just presented, that the future of the language was not in danger, someone would almost certainly question his loyalty to the community.

The imperative of a fragile and threatened nation is a dogma that can be invoked whenever there seems to be no practical solution to a social, economic, or political problem. The problem may be the language of signs, the closing of a railway line, or the decision not to bear a child. The dogma has a long history, and the threat has taken many forms. At one time it concerned Protestants and Jehovah's Witnesses. Later it was related to the issue of economic domination. Today it has to do with immigrants, birth rates, and television.

The dogma is nourished by an impressive array of arguments from diverse sources. For one group of conservative intellectuals, the most respected of whom are Léon Dion and Claude Ryan, the model is essentially the rural, Catholic society of the past. There are artists who fear that they may one day have no roots from which to draw their strength and no audience to understand what they have to say. There are individuals who have been frustrated in trying to obtain information or work in their own language. There are some who see language legislation as a useful "non-tariff barrier" that provides them with more space in their own field of activity. There are those whose ambition is the independence of Quebec and who use the language issue to promote their cause. There are sociologists, demographers, and political scientists who transform the evidence they accumulate into theories of society that place the English at the centre of the problems facing French-speaking Quebecers.

There are, as well, many thoughtful French-speaking Quebecers, with close friends in the English community, for whom, nevertheless, the words *humiliation* and *mépris* still come to mind when they think about relationships between the two communities.

The approaches may vary in detail, but they have a common theme, that of English as a danger to be opposed, based on the conviction that the two languages, in the same political space, are basically incompatible.

Where Does It End?

So we come back to the central question, posed at the beginning of this book: "Where does it all end?" If there is, someday, to be a full acceptance of a distinct English community in Quebec, there must be some consensus on the space that is to be reserved for it. One way of rephrasing the above question is to ask, "What demographic level of the English community would the French community accept as no longer posing an internal threat?" It now makes up a declining 10 percent of the population. Would 8 percent be acceptable? Would 5 percent?

The reply would probably be that the question should not be asked in this way, that the final achievement of the state of "cultural security" that Brian Mulroney and others have promised depends not on demographic statistics or any other *facts,* but on a change in attitude or in perception.

Changes in attitude and perception begin, presumably, with leaders of public opinion. At present, however, there is no one in a leadership position in French Quebec who is inclined to tell his people that they already form a strong community and are masters of their own destiny. The inescapable conclusion is that there is no political will in Quebec today to resolve the language and culture debate in a way that would explicitly accept the existence of the right of the English-speaking community to develop and grow in accordance with its own priorities, and to provide a broader range of linguistically-based rights to that community.

The provincial government and the main opposition parties compete with each other in the impossible task of bringing "cultural security" through political action to the French-speaking population. Because this commitment has been made, every French-speaking Quebecer is free to insist on the protection of his or her vision of this culture and its values. And so, all of the space in the debate is dominated by opposing views of what is fundamental to French culture and of the mechanisms that can be devised to strengthen and expand that culture.

The government, and those who influence it, can admit no limit to the expansion of French in Quebec. The Liberal Party's *present* position is that there should be an English school system with limited access, English colleges and universities, and English services provided by some health and social service institutions and in some government bodies. That is the extent of their commitment, and past experience indicates that it is subject to change. The Parti Québécois promises even less than the Liberals do.

So English Quebecers are in a quandary. They are the tangible and internal manifestation of an intangible and global problem that can seemingly never be resolved. The problem of cultural insecurity, framed in the way it is today, would not be resolved even if the English community in Quebec were to disappear completely. This means, unfortunately, that for the moment, then, English Quebecers must go about the business of strengthening their community in a climate of confrontation, or at best, of indifference.

A Better Way

The first 148 pages of this book have been spent in addressing the English-speaking community in Quebec, encouraging them to stop trying to conform to someone else's vision of society. So it may seem presumptuous now to turn to the French majority and suggest how they might more usefully understand the world around them. But the English are not alone in Quebec. They find themselves in almost daily conversation with their French-speaking neighbours. So we shall permit ourselves some brief comments on how an element of collaboration might also be added to the relationship—if the majority is so inclined.

It could be suggested that Quebec's French-speaking majority has become, in a sense, a prisoner of rhetoric that is unhelpful to them, and that there might be a better way. Considering the important and complex issues that face all Quebecers, it may well be time for the French majority to declare an end to its obsession with "English" and make good use, both of that language and the community that speaks it, for the common good.

Assume for one moment that this dogma of perpetual danger, and the confrontation with the English that it inevitably implies, is not something that people seek for its own satisfaction but is a rationally held conviction. Suppose for a moment that it is even true; that French is threatened today as never before. Let us agree that no individual has the power to face this threat alone, and therefore must rely on collective action. What is to be done?

Consider an example: the premier announces that "from every side I am receiving representations on the deterioration of the use of the language in stores."[118] But he cannot control the words people speak in stores; so, because something must be done, the government imposes unilingual signs.

But what if this does not do the job? What if people *still* speak English in stores? What is the next political step? The alternatives are too ridiculous, too painful to contemplate. The fact is—and it needs at some point to be shouted from the rooftops—no government can guarantee linguistic security to the Quebec population. The present one cannot; a government of the Parti Québécois could not; the government of an independent state of Quebec could not.

Every Quebec businessperson who has argued forcibly for free trade with the United States will understand why linguistic security cannot be guaranteed. The analogy with economic security makes it clear that protection will not make a country economically secure. It weakens the economy. Linguistic protection has the same effect. If the people of Quebec are told over and over again that French is noncompetitive except in a local context, that it needs continual protection to save it from irrelevance or disappearance, the result is to condemn it, in time, to just that.

In other words, the war against the English language in

Quebec is a sterile, unwinnable, counterproductive confrontation. It guarantees perpetual political headaches for all political parties because there is no way to win it and therefore no limit to the appetite for more and more intervention. There can be no point of equilibrium, no stopping point in the struggle. The political authorities must forever encourage the population to maintain the "ten thousand stout fellows" described by Dr. Samuel Johnson, "ready to fight against popery although they don't know if it's a man or a horse." There has to be a better way.

A Distinct Society

Many have spent much time in the past few years arguing that Quebec is a "distinct society." In its present form, this expression is used mainly as a slogan in the debate over the roles of the provincial government, the federal government, the Canadian Charter of Rights and Freedoms, and the rest of the constitution in determining how legislative responsibility is to be shared in Canada. In other words, the debate over the meaning of "distinct society" is part of a debate about political power. A moment's reflection, however, makes it clear that the only reason for engaging in a constitutional struggle over the meaning of "distinct society" is to put the results to work in order to build a better future.

What is it for? Is Quebec distinct in any way, apart from the fact that most of the population speaks French? What is it that Quebec has to say in that language? This question is pertinent for all who believe that a language, although important, is finally only a means of communication and certainly not worth dying for.

Is a single language necessary to permit people to express themselves fully? Some Quebecers, particularly artists, say that they can only be themselves, truly "live," in their *own* language. This argument, however, rings hollow when immigrants to Quebec are urged to abandon their native languages in order to "integrate" into French or English.

For most people, the language they use is simply *not* a life-or-death issue. A new thought, like a silly remark, can be expressed in any language. Some excellent work has been done by people all over the world in a language that was not their mother tongue. Samuel Beckett, an Irishman, and Eugene Ionesco, a Romanian, are only two examples of artists who had something of importance to say in French, even though it was not their first language. Joseph Conrad, a Pole, did not speak English until the age of twenty, but he managed to do some work in that language that is still appreciated today. On a more mundane level, many English-speaking Quebecers—and I am one of them—have worked for many years in French without any evident damage to our souls.

Considering what is happening in other parts of the world today—Europe is an interesting example—it is possible to speculate that within the next fifty years, language, which has for the moment replaced religion as the unifying element in Quebec society, will itself come to be seen as equally irrelevant in defining what Quebecers really are.

After asking *what* the distinct society is for, it might be worth asking *who* it is intended to benefit. Within Quebec who, precisely, is doing what to whom in this debate? Who are the winners and the losers in the drive for a totally French Quebec—businesspeople, workers, the economy, bureaucrats, inventors, artists, athletes? Or is this a unique phenomenon in which every French Quebecer emerges a winner?

The question is worth pondering because French Quebec will not make itself happy or prosperous, nor will it make any contribution to the welfare of this planet, simply because it speaks French. Exactly the same is true for English Quebec. Everyone has a right to ask, where in the world is Quebec going?

With these questions in mind, it is worth examining another possible relationship between the two main language groups in Quebec: co-operation based on self-confidence.

Let us accept for a moment that English in Quebec is here to stay. The English-speaking community, a distinct society in Quebec, present in the voices of individuals and institutions almost since the first Europeans arrived in this territory, is now a real community. Space must be found for it, an accommodation must be reached, whatever political form Quebec chooses for itself in the future. Quebec has always been French—and English—and it still is.

The English community in Quebec, aware of both its minority status and its collective responsibility, seeks recognition, accommodation, and agreement on a relationship with the French-speaking majority that will be beneficial to both parties and make it possible for Quebec to define itself in terms that have new relevance for both Canada and the world. This approach requires collaboration, not confrontation.

What form can this co-operation take? First, it requires acceptance by both sides, an acceptance sanctioned and informed by the government, that success for the English Quebecer or the French Quebecer in this world is a victory for all. The English community has made important contributions to the life of Quebec, *while working in English in Quebec*—and it wants to continue to do so.

Its contributions are not limited to business and the Montreal Neurological Institute. Mordecai Richler's and Leonard Cohen's successes in the world are—like those of Michel Tremblay and Denys Arcand—Quebec success stories. One doesn't have to agree with everything they say to recognize them as artists, and the fact that their message can be translated does not diminish the language in which it was first written. On the contrary.

Could we all possibly become a little more relaxed about our need for linguistic and cultural distinctiveness and celebrate, in the words of Salman Rushdie, the "inevitable polyglot world" of "hybridity, impurity, intermingling, the transformation that comes of new and unexpected combinations of human beings, cultures, ideas, politics, movies, songs," rejoice in "mongrelization" and fear "the absolutism of the Pure"?[119] In other words, might Quebec not now join the immediate future, and do it better than many more homogeneous societies that know only one way of life?

We can speak other languages for a variety of reasons, but above all so that we can communicate with each other. We may not like each other better as a result, but at least we will understand more clearly that a variety of perspectives exists. In tolerating and encouraging bilingualism, Quebecers can perhaps be tolerant and understanding of those who speak only one language and learn to respect their plans for their own lives—or their lack of plans. We can begin in North America a small version of the difficult but essential work that began forty years ago in Europe—the reconciliation of various cultural groups in a spirit of mutual respect, with the goal of better understanding, greater prosperity, and an end to the kind of conflict that has set back humanity and exposed the destructive side of mankind since the beginning of time.

In Quebec, the first steps have been taken. The French have now grown strong, even if their leaders hesitate to confirm it. There is no more need to be defensive. At the same time, the English community, once seen as a dangerous but undefinable adversary of French Quebec, has materialized. It exists as a distinct minority community, with a new leadership and a commitment to a Quebec that it would have a part in defining.

There is important news today for French-speaking Quebecers who are willing to listen. English Quebecers are not their enemies. They are no more powerful, no richer, no more arrogant, no more intolerant, no less concerned about the future of Quebec than French Quebecers are. Language legislation has been taken as far as it can go; French Quebec has succeeded in business; the provincial government is its exclusive preserve. Yet its leaders still persist in telling Quebecers that the English are dangerous.

We are not dangerous; we are determined to remain and grow and are more organized than ever before. But we are not organized for confrontation, only to ensure our own future. Surely French Quebecers can understand that attitude, because we learned it from them. We want them to believe that we are not a threat to the province's culture, but an asset.

The day Brian Mulroney referred to, when Quebec's "cultural security" is achieved, will not come about by a decision of the Office de la Langue Française or as the result of some new statistics, or even by a unilateral declaration of independence. It will arrive when Quebec's leaders decide that the time has come to start telling the people that they are strong.

Why not today? Why not "put another movie in our heads," right now? Why not start today with the premise that French-speaking Quebecers are *now* possessed of enough personal and collective self-confidence to accept the English for what they are: a minority group whose political strength in the province is limited, but who are Quebecers in their own way, who intend to remain there, and who can make useful and agreeable partners. We are—let's admit it—friends who have known each other for a long time.

Peace

To carry this vision a little further, let us imagine for a moment that the day has come when the members of the French-speaking majority in Quebec are prepared to say this to their English-speaking neighbours:

> You are the second-language community of Quebec, and we hope you grow stronger, in English. We accept your right to be Quebecers in a way that you and no one else will define.
>
> We support your right to your own institutions, run in the way you would like to run them, within the limits of the administrative constraints and the limited resources to which we are all subject.
>
> Speak English in Quebec, where and when you wish. We intend to speak French, and when we talk together we will speak whichever language enables us to understand each other.

You are not just another cultural community. English is not just another language. It is the second language of Quebec and much more than that. We accept this, and it doesn't bother us. It is a fact of life, and we are at ease with it.

We intend to live and work in French, and we make up nearly all of the population here. So, if you want to participate fully in Quebec life, you had better learn it too. But if you don't want to, you are still welcome here. It's your life. Quebec is not a language; it is a place where you can feel free to live and develop in your own way. If you wish to make your contribution to our Quebec in English, that's fine with us.

We propose a civil relationship between all our inhabitants, regardless of where they came from or when they arrived, and we recognize that they are not here primarily to realize some grand collective design but to live their lives as they see fit.

The purpose of language legislation for us is not to create a new "people," but simply to ensure that the vast majority of our citizens can express themselves publicly in the tongue they use privately. We will employ it, not to make a point about who is "boss," but as a practical regulatory tool to achieve certain objectives. We will seek agreement with you on measures to protect the French language because, for most of you, it is now one of your languages too.

Whatever the English may have been for us in the past is no longer pertinent today. Everything you do, we can do as well or better. The English have no power over us, and to pretend that they do does not make us stronger or better. It diminishes us and condemns us to a useless inferiority. We will ignore those among us who would fight old battles, which have already been won, with the vocabulary of the eternal loser.

We face the uncertainties of the future, which are

156

shared by all the world's people, with confidence. Some of the people who come to Quebec in the years ahead will speak English; so be it. More will speak French, because it is the main language of Quebec, and we will show them that they can be successful and happy here, in French.

So far as your English community is concerned, we recognize the validity of your preoccupations, including the commitments made to you from 1978 to 1985, and we think they are reasonable. Let's renegotiate them now.

In conclusion, we tell you without apprehension that Quebec, our unique home in North America, is and can remain French, and English too. Let's get on with our lives.

If this day has arrived—and we have been promised that it will arrive—then another, more interesting book than this one must now be written.

If not, please return to Chapter Five.

NOTES

1 The size of Quebec's English community cannot be established with absolute precision. Since 1971, the Canadian census has asked two questions relating to language in an effort to establish: (1) *mother tongue,* the language first spoken and still understood; and (2) *home language,* the language most frequently used in the home.

Since 1981, multiple answers to the two questions have been recorded. A person may declare that he or she has two or more "mother tongues" or "home languages." The following table, prepared by Statistics Canada, includes an allocation of these multiple responses to provide optimum consistency in comparing year-to-year changes.

The total figure for the home language population is smaller than for mother tongue because a slightly different base is used. The mother tongue statistics correspond to the total population figures used by Statistics Canada for other purposes. Unless otherwise specified, these are the figures used in this book.

Linguistic Distribution of the Population of Quebec

MOTHER TONGUE (in thousands)

	1971		1976		1981		1986	
French	4,867	80.7	4,989	80.0	5,307	82.4	5,409	82.8
English	789	13.1	801	12.9	706	11.0	679	10.4
Other	371	6.2	445	7.1	425	6.6	445	6.8
Total	6,027	100.0	6,235	100.0	6,438	100.0	6,533	100.0

HOME LANGUAGE (in thousands)

	1971		1976		1981		1986	
French	4,870	80.8	N/A		5,257	82.5	5,343	82.8
English	889	14.7	N/A		809	12.7	797	12.3
Other	270	4.5	N/A		303	4.8	315	4.9
Total	6,029	100.0	N/A		6,369	100.0	6,455	100.0

Source: Language Unit, Housing, Family and Social Statistics Division, Statistics Canada, June 5, 1990.

2 *Commission of Inquiry on the Position of the French Language and on Language Rights in Quebec* (Gendron Commission), (Quebec: Éditeur Officiel du Québec, 1972).

3 In 1983, the Parti Québécois made some minor amendments to the law (Bill 57) to correct a number of injustices and contradictions. Among the most important of these changes was one that permitted "institutional bilingualism" in the English health and social services institutions.

4 Government of Canada, *Report of the Task Force on Canadian Unity* (Pepin–Robarts Report), (Ottawa, 1979).

5 Statistics Canada, cat. no. 91-210; Luc Albert, "Language in Canada," *Canadian Social Trends,* No. 12, Spring 1989.

6 *Le Soleil,* February 2, 1979.

7 In 1989, unable to find a suitable candidate in the riding of Westmount because of opposition to Bill 178, the Liberals nominated William Cosgrove, an employee of the World Bank, then residing in Washington, D.C. He lost to the Equality Party candidate.

8 William Shaw was elected in the riding of Pointe Claire for the Union Nationale, largely because this party promised "freedom of choice" in the educational sector. When the leader of the Union Nationale changed his position on this issue a few months later, Shaw resigned from the Union Nationale caucus and sat as an independent member.

9 Dr. Goldbloom resigned shortly after Claude Ryan was elected leader of the Liberal Party.

10 Claude Ryan, "Déclaration de Claude Ryan sur La Politique Linguistique," April 1978.

11 *Montreal Star,* February 15, 1979.

12 Resolution No. 5, adopted by the General Council of the Liberal Party of Quebec in June 1985 on the basis of powers deferred to it by the party congress.

13 Claude Ryan, "Letter to My Fellow-Citizens of Notre-Dame-de-Grâce," June 27, 1978. Essentially the same letter was written to the voters in the riding of Argenteuil on April 16, 1979, during the by-election in which Ryan was the Liberal candidate.

14 Speech by Claude Ryan, leader of the Liberal Party of Quebec, in Ville Saint-Pierre, June 28, 1978.

15 Speech given on radio station CJMS and published as "Le

francais, langue obligatoire dans l'affichage au Québec," in *La Presse,* December 2, 1986.

16 Quoted by Donald Charette, "Bourassa est prêt à permettre l'affichage bilingue très bientôt," *Le Devoir,* October 4, 1986.

17 Gendron Report, Recommendation 73.

18 Charter of the French Language, section 58.

19 *Ford c. Procurer général du Québec,* [1985] C.S. 147.

20 Quoted by Rollande Parent, "Affichage: Bourassa ne dit pas non à une commission parlementaire," *Le Devoir,* October 18, 1986.

21 Gilles Lesage, "Bourassa peut permettre l'affichage bilingue sans même passer par l'Assemblée nationale," *Le Devoir,* October 16, 1986.

22 Report of the "groupe de travail technique" presided by Pierre-Étienne Laporte, submitted to the minister of cultural affairs in two parts, on December 11 and 19, 1986.

23 *Procurer général du Québec c. La Chaussure Brown's Inc.,* [1987] R.J.Q. 80 (C.A.).

24 Sarah Scott, "Quebec Likely to Appeal Sign-Law Ruling: Marx," Montreal *Gazette,* January 22, 1987.

25 See, for example, the premier's exclusive interview with Mike Cohen and Martin Stone in *The Suburban,* January 13, 1988.

26 *Ford v. Attorney General of Quebec,* [1988] 2 S.C.R. 712.

27 The "notwithstanding clause" may only be applied to sections 2 and 7–15 of the Charter. Bill 178 also contained a clause enabling it to override the Quebec Charter of Human Rights and Freedoms.

28 Sarah Scott, "More Restrictions Added to Sign Law," Montreal *Gazette,* December 22, 1988.

29 Nancy Wood, "Law 'Barely Changes' Bill 101: Premier," Montreal *Gazette,* December 24, 1988.

30 Assemblée Nationale du Québec, *Journal des débats,* December 20, 1988, p. 4430.

31 Ibid., p. 4439.

32 Ibid., p. 4418.

33 The Meech Lake Agreement is the popular name for the constitutional amendments approved unanimously by the first ministers of Canada at their meeting in Ottawa on June 2 and 3, 1987. The project was abandoned in June 1990 because two provincial premiers failed to have the agreement ratified by their legislatures within the three-year time limit.

34 A few days after the adoption of Bill 178, a fire broke out in the offices of Alliance Quebec. For several days a rumour of unknown origin circulated in the news media to the effect that Royal Orr had set the fire to discredit the French-speaking community. After several days' delay, the police investigated and declared there was no foundation to this rumour.

35 Assemblée Nationale du Québec, *Journal des débats*, December 20, 1988, p. 4452.

36 Ibid., pp. 4450–51.

37 Resolution adopted at a special meeting of the General Council of the Liberal Party of Quebec, December 17, 1988.

38 Lysiane Gagnon, "Un jugement contestable," *La Presse*, December 17, 1988. Those who were willing to debate the matter with her at this level noted that the case had, in fact, been heard by eleven judges during its progress through the three courts. Seven of these eleven judges were French speaking. The decision was unanimous in each case.

39 One of the more moderate expressions of this point of view can be found in an article by Jean-Louis Bourque, "Il faut refuser la guerre des chartes," *La Presse*, December 21, 1988.

40 Chambre de Commerce du Québec, *Communiqué*, December 22, 1988; Conseil du Patronat du Québec, *Communiqué*, December 20, 1988.

41 "Le français partout," *Le Devoir*, December 17, 1988.

42 A prominent member of the board of directors of *Le Devoir*, Marcel Pépin, resigned the following day in protest against Benoit Lauzière's position: Irwin Block, "Pépin Quits Le Devoir to Protest Editorial," Montreal *Gazette*, December 18, 1988.

43 Sorécom poll for *Le Soleil*.

44 See note 33.

45 Claude Ryan, "Reconciliation: A Quebec View," speech given at Queen's University, Kingston, Ontario, December 8, 1989.

46 See the intervention of the attorney general of Quebec in the case of *Mahe et al.* before the Supreme Court of Canada, June 1989 (appeal no. 20590).

47 Quoted by Bernard Descôteaux, "Pas question de traiter les universités 'sur un pied aveuglément arithmetique,'" *Le Devoir*, October 18, 1989.

48 Bill 142, amending the Health and Social Services Act, was adopted in December 1986.

49 See "Brief Presented to the Parliamentary Committee on the Budget and Administration Regarding the Public Service Act, R.S.Q., c. F-3.1.1 by Alliance Quebec" (September 1990).

50 Liste des sous-ministres et des sous-ministres adjoints; Réforme administrative et Emplois supérieurs, January 12, 1990.

51 Liste d'adresses des dirigeants ou personnes contacts des organismes gouvernementaux; Le Secrétariat à la réforme administrative et au emplois supérieurs, October 30, 1989.

52 Montreal *Gazette,* August 28, 1989.

53 Bill 58, An Act Respecting the Eligibility of Certain Children for Instruction in English, introduced May 15, 1986.

54 Bill 140, An Act to Amend the Charter of the French Language, introduced November 13, 1986. The law was never adopted.

55 Bill 142, An Act to Modify the Law regarding Health and Social Services, tabled November 12, 1986.

56 *Report on the Affairs of British North America* (Durham Report), British Parliamentary Papers, London, 1839.

57 Only the Liberal ridings of Charlevoix, Montmagny-L'Islet, Jean Talon, Maskinonge, Portneuf, Roberval, and Shefford had populations in which fewer than 10 percent were English-speaking.

58 See, for example, the comments of J. Roméo Brault on the change in Ryan's position: Montreal *Gazette,* January 7, 1982.

59 "Maitrisons L'Avenir," Commission Politique, Liberal Party of Quebec, February 1985. The English member was John Trent, a member of the faculty of the University of Ottawa.

60 See the editorial "Courage Seems Mixed" in the Montreal *Gazette,* February 7, 1985.

61 In these thirty counties, there was a non-French-speaking population of at least 10 percent.

62 Quoted by Denis Lessard, *La Presse,* December 19, 1988.

63 "La Langue D'Affichage au Québec; L'État de L'Opinion Publique Selon les Principaux Sondages Depuis 1979," Sorécom Inc., October 1986.

64 "Quebec's Premier Says Limiting the Use of English Will Not Deter Investors," *Financial Times of Canada,* April 24, 1989.

65 See, for example, Brendan O'Donnell, *Printed Sources for the*

Study of English-Speaking Quebec: An Annotated Bibliography of Works Printed Before 1980, Eastern Townships Research Centre Series, No. 2 (Lennoxville: Bishop's University, 1985). This bibliography lists 2,698 references.

66 See Ronald Rudin, *The Forgotten Quebecers: A History of English-Speaking Quebec 1759–1980,* chapter 6, "The Changing Ethnic Composition of English Quebec" (IQRC, 1985). Mr. Rudin's figures, quoted here, are based on the 1981 census.

67 See note 115.

68 See François Vaillancourt and Josée Carpentier, *Le contrôle de l'économie du Québec: La place des francophones en 1987 et son évolution depuis 1961* (Québec: CDRE Office de la langue française, July 1989). Table 2.2.B on page 20 indicates that in 1987, jobs in the manufacturing sector were controlled by 226,363 francophone Canadians, 219,920 anglophone Canadians, and 129,517 non-Canadians.

69 See, for example, Edouard Cloutier, "What's In a Name? Problems of Group Identity in Quebec," in *The English of Quebec: From Majority to Minority Status,* edited by Gary Caldwell and Eric Waddell (IQRC, 1982).

70 Luc Albert, "Language in Canada," *Canadian Social Trends,* No. 12, Spring 1989.

71 Ibid.

72 See, for example, the editorial by Alain Dubuc, "Les anglophones ont-ils une place au Québec?" *La Presse,* May 31, 1989.

73 Elie Kedourie, in *Nationalism* (London: Hutchison, reprinted 1986), says that "nationalism is a doctrine invented in Europe at the beginning of the 19th century." K.R. Minogue, in *Nationalism* (London: Methuen, 1967), points to the French Revolution as the moment at which the concept finally arrived on "firm ground."

74 See Minogue, ibid.

75 See, for example, section 93 of the *Constitution Act, 1867.*

76 See note 46.

77 The Universal Declaration of Human Rights was adopted by the General Assembly of the United Nations on December 10, 1948.

78 Assemblée Nationale du Québec, *Journal des débats,* July 19, 1977.

79 "S'indigner ou ne pas s'indigner," *La Presse,* January 7, 1989.

80 Statistics Canada census figures, quoted in Gilles Grenier, "Bilingualism among Anglophones and Francophones in Canada," in "Demolinguistic Trends and the Evolution of Canadian Institutions," special issue of the *Canadian Issues* series of the Association for Canadian Studies, Montreal, 1989.

81 David Johnston, "The Price of Learning English: No First Communion for Kids," Montreal *Gazette*, April 9, 1989.

82 See note 115.

83 Lord Halifax, quoted by Michael Oakeshott in a remarkable passage (pp. 236–39) of his book *On Human Conduct* (Oxford: Oxford University Press, 1975). Professor Oakeshott would almost certainly find my present effort at political activism to be, at best, a little irrelevant. But I have felt him looking over my shoulder every step of the way, and whatever good there may be in this book is, in no small measure, due to his influence.

84 The English-language vote in the election was analysed by Pierre Drouilly in "Le succès des Partis égalité et unité," *Le Devoir*, October 4, 1989.

85 *Elections Québec 1989: Rapport Préliminaire Résultats des Élections*, Le Directeur général des élections du Québec, October 12, 1989.

86 Charter of the French Language, section 4.

87 For an interesting look at the present state of language regulation in the workplace, especially its ambiguity and legislative limits, see Emmanuel Didier, "Private Law of Language," chapter 6 of *Language Rights in Canada*, edited by Michel Bastarache et al. (Montreal: Les Editions Yvon Blais Inc., 1987). Part III of this chapter, "The Law of Business Communications," deals directly with the subject.

88 *La répartition de la population selon la langue maternelle pour les circonscriptions électorales du Québec*, Le Directeur général des élections du Québec, May 1990.

89 Information supplied by Statistics Canada based on 1986 census.

90 *Source*: Statistics Canada. The Montreal Region, as defined by Statistics Canada, is somewhat larger than the Montreal Urban Community and had a total population of 2,921,355 in 1986. The figures shown for the city of Montreal do not include multiple responses.

91 *Profil Socio-economique de L'Arrondissement Centre* (Service Planification Concertation, Montreal, March 1989).

92 John Ciaccia, the minister of international affairs, speech given

to the Canadian Business Club of Seoul, South Korea, May 31, 1990. See also the book by Marc V. Levine referred to in note 115. The title speaks for itself.

93 For an analysis of the birth rates of English and French Quebecers, see Réjean Lachapelle, "Changes in Fertility Among Canada's Linguistic Groups," *Canadian Social Trends,* No. 10, Autumn 1988.

94 *Données préliminaires sur l'immigration du 4ème trimestre 1989 et de l'année 1989,* Ministère des Communautés culturelles et de l'Immigration, March 26, 1990.

95 Some examples at the time of writing were: Michael Goldbloom, president of the Ville Marie Social Service Centre; Eric Maldoff, president of the Montreal Children's Hospital; Vaughan Dowie, president of the Youth Protection Commission; Alex Paterson, chairman of McGill University; Thomas Mulcair, president of the Office of Professions; Russell Williams, member of the National Assembly; and John Parisella, executive assistant to the premier of Quebec.

96 The most recent document summarizing the cultural institutions of the English community in Quebec is *Working Papers on English Language Institutions in Quebec,* edited by Susan Schachter and published by Alliance Quebec in March 1982. Much of the information in the following paragraphs is based on working paper IV, "Culture," of this document.

97 "Watch Your Language," speech given at Trent University, Peterborough, Ontario, March 8, 1989.

98 It is generally agreed that the health and social service sector requires important reforms, and a number of steps have been taken in this direction in recent years. The Rochon Commission presented its report in 1988, and in 1989 and 1990 the minister of social affairs held public hearings on possible changes to the structures, mandates, and financing of these institutions.

99 Gendron Report, recommendation 72. In Finland, a commune is considered bilingual if the minority-language group exceeds 8 percent of the population or consists of at least three thousand people. A bilingual commune becomes unilingual when the minority-language group falls below 6 percent. *Source:* Svenska Finlands Folkting, Helsinki, 1989.

100 Charter of the French Language, section 113*f.*

101 In 1989, the town of Rosemère contested in court the decision

of the Office of the French Language to remove the bilingual status of this community because its non-French population had dropped below the required 50 percent level. A decision of the Quebec Superior Court in August 1990 held that the Office of the French Language, relying on only one set of figures from Statistics Canada, had not *proved* that the English population was below the required level. The bilingual status of Rosemère was reinstated but the principle that a majority was required in order to maintain bilingual status was not put in question.

102 See note 88.

103 Among the many efforts made to separate "liberals" from "conservatives," see "Ideas About Freedom," Occasional Paper No. 15 (St. Leonards, N.S.W., Australia: Centre for Independent Studies, 1986).

104 See note 89.

105 Quoted by Paul Koring, "PM Says Francophones' Pain Outweighs Anglophone Rights," *The Globe and Mail,* September 23, 1989.

106 "The Mystery of Quebec," *Daedalus* (The American Academy of Arts and Sciences), Vol. 117, No. 4, Fall 1988, at p. 290.

107 "Pour sauver notre langue," *Le Soleil,* April 10, 1989.

108 Policy document of the Liberal Party of Quebec, adopted at the General Council meeting, June 4, 1989; quoted by Robert McKenzie, "Quebec Liberals Sounding a Lot Like Parti Québécois," *Toronto Star,* June 3, 1989.

109 "La tentation de la séparation," *Le Soleil,* June 28, 1989.

110 *Annual Report of the Commissioner for Official Languages, 1988* (Ottawa, 1988), quoted by William Johnson, "Paranoia Mars Talk of 'Threat' to French" Montreal *Gazette,* April 12, 1989.

111 Cedric May, "Towards the Vernacular: The Slow Validation of Popular Culture in Francophone Canada," Canada House Lecture Series No. 43 (London, 1988).

112 Sylvain Blanchard, "Le président de la Chambre du Québec s'inquiète du poids démographique des Québécois de souche," *Le Devoir,* November 18, 1989.

113 See note 106.

114 See Brian Young and John A. Dickinson, *A Short History of Quebec: A Socio-Economic Perspective* (Toronto: Copp Clark Pitman Ltd., 1988), p. 110.

115 See Jean-Marc Lévesque, "Bilingualism and Earnings" in *Per-*

spectives on Labour and Income (Government of Canada, Minister of Regional Industrial Expansion, Summer 1989), and an analysis of this and other related documents by Claude Picher in *La Presse,* June 3, 1989. See also the recently published *The Reconquest of Montreal: Language Policy and Social Change in a Bilingual City* by Marc V. Levine (Philadelphia: Temple University Press, 1990). Note especially pp. 195–99.

116 Ministère des Communautés culturelles et de l'Immigration, *Bulletin statistique annuelle,* Vol. 13, 1986 et 1987 (Quebec: MCCI, 1989).

117 "La langue d'accueil et la langue de service dans les commerces de Montréal," *Bulletin du Conseil de la Langue Francaise,* Vol. 6, No. 2, Printemps 1989.

118 Quoted by Denis Lessard, "Le français langue de service se détériore, admet Bourassa," *La Presse,* December 21, 1988.

119 Salman Rushdie, "In Good Faith," *The Independent* (London), February 4, 1990.

INDEX